"This is a powerful, moving book that shows you how to draw upon the deep reserves of strength and determination that lie within you - and take control of your life."

—Brian Tracy
Speaker, Author, Consultant
Author of *Goals!*

"This book will nurture your soul and nourish your mind with inspiring and heartwarming stories about real life journeys of adversity that often create relational & spiritual abundance. A great read!"

—Nido Qubein
Chairman, Great Harvest Bread Company
Founder, National Speakers Association Foundation

"A phenomenal and uplifting collection of stories by cancer survivors, ***Make Your Own Miracle: Surviving Cancer*** *will show you the strength and power that hope, positive thinking and a 'winning attitude' can have on conquering this insidious disease. If you or someone you care about has cancer, this book is for you."*

—Robert G. Allen
Four-time NY Times best-selling author
Co-author of the blockbuster *The One Minute Millionaire: The Enlightened Way to Wealth* with Mark Victor Hansen

"A deeply profound and personally motivating collection of stories. Many of us with cancer can survive, and many of us will survive if we face the challenge with such positive energy and trust in the future."

—Kevin Sharpe
Oxford University, Union Institute & University, founder *Science & Spirit* magazine
Author of *Sleuthing the Divine*, and (forthcoming) *Love and Happiness*

Make Your Own Miracle™: Surviving Cancer

By Paul Huff

With Julie Valeant Yenichek and Kim Huff

Southern Mountains Press

Make Your Own Miracle™: Surviving Cancer

Southern Mountains Press/January 2005

The purpose of this book is to educate, entertain, and to assist people and businesses. It is not intended or suggested that it be used for any other reasons. It is sold with the understanding that the author is not a physician and that neither the author nor the publisher are engaged in providing legal, medical or financial advice.The book should be used only as a general guide and not as the ultimate source of information on the subjects covered and legal or advice should be obtained from an attorney or physician. Thus the author and the publisher specifically disclaim any liability for loss or damage alleged to be caused directly or indirectly by using the information in this book.

ISBN:
0-9723963-4-9

Library of Congress Control Number: 2004115073

Cover Design: Greg Russell

The author, Paul Huff, is available for consultations, seminars and speaking engagements. Contact him at: www.paulhuff.com.

To find out more about Make Your Own Miracle™ programs or to post your story, visit our website: www.makeyourownmiracle.com.

DEDICATION

From the Edge

Come to the edge.
No, we will fall.

Come to the edge.
No, we will fall.

They came to the edge.
He pushed them and they flew.

—Guillaume Appolinaire

This book is dedicated to the many survivors who have stood "at the edge," overcame the odds and re-engaged stronger than ever with life. Fifty-five of their stories are included in this book.

Make Your Own Miracle™: Surviving Cancer

Acknowledgments

This book took more than two years from conception to completion. As we began to think about all the people to whom we would like to express our deepest appreciation for their support, suggestions and hard work in making this book possible, we realized that this labor of love took the combined efforts of many people. We especially wish to acknowledge the following:

Joyce Thomas, whose editorial contributions to this book were absolutely invaluable. Thank you, Joyce! We couldn't have done it without you. You "felt" the stories as much as we did, and that was evident in your work.

Larry Chilnick, for your expertise in every facet of getting this book done. You caught the vision for the *Make Your Own Miracle*™ brand, and kept the processing and flow of the material working all along. Thanks for believing in the book, Larry.

Jim Norman, who is Paul's friend and mentor. Thanks for your ongoing wisdom, insight and friendship. I know I can always count on you for the "truth."

Patti Schaar, who helped with research in connection with the stories.

Larry Burnham, whose last minute editorial contribution made a significant difference to the finished product.

All the people, who originally sent in stories or relapsed during the project. While we could not include everything we received, we were touched by *all* the stories.

Finally, Julie would also like to thank her family and friends for all their support with this project, especially her husband, Tony, who spent countless hours reading and listening to stories. In addition, Julie thanks Phyllis Valeant, Ruth Yenichek, Joel Stephens and Jim "Philly" Strain, who inspired her to work for the American Cancer Society.

Cancer is So Limited

It cannot cripple love
It cannot shatter hope
It cannot corrode faith
It cannot destroy peace
It cannot kill friendship
It cannot suppress memories
It cannot silence courage
It cannot invade the soul
It cannot steal eternal life
It cannot conquer the spirit

—Source Unknown

To find out more about Make Your Own Miracle™ programs or to post your story, visit our website: www.makeyourownmiracle.com.

Contents

Resources:

Introduction

Make Your Own Miracle

"There are two ways to live your life. One is as though nothing is a miracle. The other is as though everything is."

—Albert Einstein

According to a 2003 Harris Poll, 84% of Americans believe in miracles. Personally, and for as long as I can remember, I have always been fascinated by the concept of miracles. To my mind, a miracle can be an act of divine intervention or simply an event that can't be explained by normal or scientific means.

You are about to read 55 stories of cancer patients who made their own miracles. Many were given a 10% or less chance to survive. Yet, they defied the odds and came back not just strong, but stronger. Who are they and why did they survive? Why did they make it when 90% sadly succumb? What role did they play in creating their own personal miracles? Was there a common thread of faith or medical care?

Because of my personal story, I wanted to know theirs, and I wanted to hear those stories in their own words. I wanted to know because my wife was one of those who did not beat the odds. Later, I found that others with cancer, and those who cared about and for them, were also searching for those answers…were also searching for help and information from those who defied the worst this dreaded disease has to offer.

Friday, November 28, 1986 stands out forever in my memory. It was the Friday after Thanksgiving—the day my wife of 19 years was diagnosed with a malignant tumor. If you or someone close to you has ever heard the words "You have cancer," you *know* what I felt that day.

Within two weeks of her initial diagnosis, we heard two even graver words: metastatic melanoma. About this diagnosis our oncologist said, "There is no cure. I suggest you get your affairs in order." He looked directly at my wife and said, "You probably have six months to live."

Sadly, my wife Janice lived only two months longer than that dreaded prediction. During those eight months, she displayed a powerful willingness to get well. She showed incredible courage as she endured immense physical pain after mammoth doses of chemotherapy.

Even as I admired and respected Janice's tenacity, I still felt a critical piece of the puzzle for her survival was missing: her attitude. To be more precise, I would call it her "sense of positive expectancy." The little hope she had dwindled on a daily basis. My heart sank one afternoon when I heard her tell a nurse, "All the hope I have could fit inside a tiny thimble."

What could I do to help with this missing piece? Indeed, it's my natural inclination to help people transform their thinking. Success in my chosen career as a speaker, seminar leader and executive coach hinges on my ability to find and communicate solutions in a way that causes people to think, believe and act differently.

More than ever, I was determined to deal with this missing piece, the miracle I knew she needed. During Janice's illness, I studied everything I could. I read "Getting Well Again" by O. Carl Simonton, M.D. Like a man possessed, I tore through Laurence LeShan's "Cancer as a Turning Point." I listened to Louise Hay's self-help audio recordings. Late into the night, I read passages to Janice from the best of what I was learning about attitude and cancer survival. Before I left the hospital each evening, I pressed "play" on the cassette player I had placed on her hospital tray, leaving Louise Hay or Norman Cousins to be the voice of hope when I couldn't be there.

Apparently, my actions created a stir at this reportedly progressive hospital. Janice's nurses scolded me often saying, "You're only giving her false hope. You have no right to do that." False hope? No right? Distaining the criticism, I kept pushing, prodding, encouraging and even cajoling Janice to hope. To believe in miracles. To think that survival really was possible.

I know that experts are divided on the role that attitude or a patient's state of mind plays in healing and recovery. There are many who say attitude cannot overcome biology while others, especially those who have added their stories to the literature of hope in this book, don't really dwell on scientific theories. They know what they've experienced. And I am solidly in their camp.

Even though Janice did not survive, what I learned during her illness convinced me that attitude *does* play a critical role in success. I learned that while *wanting to live* is essential, it is not enough. Having the *courage to fight* is also essential, but it's still not enough. Survival, particularly against-the-odds survival, depends on these three things:

Hope—the foundational emotion, which can lead to...

Belief—knowing you are bigger than your current situation, which can lead to...

Certainty—when you truly expect to win.

Hope—Anyone who tells a cancer patient "there is no hope" makes a tragic mistake. That person clearly does not understand the magical power of the human spirit.

One expert, Ann Webster, Ph.D., Program Director of the Cancer and Successful Aging Program at the Mind/Body Medical Institute run by The Harvard Medical School says this:

> "Being optimistic... certainly has an impact on the quality of life. If you are optimistic and hopeful and have that fighting spirit, you will go through the whole cancer experience in a much better way than if you are depressed and hopeless."

Belief—The Law of Belief states that whatever we sincerely believe begins to manifest itself in our lives. History is filled with examples of strong belief overcoming the seemingly impossible. We've seen it everywhere from playing fields to battlefields. Henry Ford said it well. "Whether you think you can, or you think you can't—either way you're right."

Certainty—Most people understand Belief at a conscious level. It is getting to the deeper, unconscious level that proves challenging. *Wanting to believe* is a long distance from *having a sense of certainty* on the continuum of success. I know that certainty, that sense of positive expectancy, was the missing piece for Janice.

You never know what can lead to a miracle.

For thousands of years, no one had been able to run a mile in under four minutes. Yet, when Roger Bannister did it in 1954, more and more athletes started to do the same. Why? Bannister broke the *psychological* barrier. Those athletes always had the physical abilities, but they had been limited by their beliefs! With Bannister's success, they developed a new belief of their own:

"If he can do it, I **can** do it."

That principle is the driving force behind this book. It is my wish that, through these stories of love, hope, belief and perseverance, you can be among those who say with certainty:

"If they can do it, I **will** do it."

In peace, love and healing,

Paul Huff

To find out more about Make Your Own Miracle™ programs or to post your story, visit our website: www.makeyourownmiracle.com.

Common Threads

By Paul Huff

When I first read the death-defying success stories that define "Make Your Own Miracle™," I was overwhelmed by the riveting honesty and raw courage of each account. I became a man driven. I wanted to know **WHY** these people—a diverse cross section of individuals from every walk of life, from around the world, whose struggles with cancer began as early as age 7 or as late as age 82, with some affording the finest care and others depending on the generosity of family and friends—ALL survived and thrived?

Despite their ethnic, cultural, financial and generational diversity, did common threads exist that allowed them to make it, while 90% or more of those with similar cancers did not? What did they have? What did they do? What did they feel? In other words, what went into the making of these miracles?

I hoped I would find a motif that screamed loud and clear, "Here it is! Do this and everything will be fine." Naturally I found no one answer, no one right way. However, I did discover common threads running through most of these accounts. These threads can serve as guideposts when dealing with the most vile, life-threatening cancers.

- **Relentless Commitment to Survival:** One common thread in nearly all of these stories is a total refusal to give up despite the opinion of experts, despite the pain and suffering, despite looking death squarely in the eye. All of these cancer survivors in one way or another said "yes" to life time and again, and it wasn't mere lip service. They said "yes" from the heart and from the soul. And they said it with commitment and certainty. They WOULD defy the odds and survive.

- **Clarity of Purpose**: People who win, whether at professional sports or a battle with cancer, have their eyes on the ball. They are singularly focused on the goal. Everything else takes second or third place to the main objective. Many of our cancer survivors displayed that unwavering clarity of purpose as they fought for their lives. Whether incorporating alternative protocols into their treatments, seeking second and third medical opinions or simply living *as if* they were already OK, they stayed focused and got well.

- **Belief in a Higher Source of Power:** The clear majority of our cancer survivors found solace in prayer and thanksgiving. In seeking the help of a higher power and asking others to do the same, they often found the strength to go on and the belief they would be healed. Many see their recovery as a miracle from God, accompanied by a commitment to help others as they continue on in life.

- **A Definably Positive Attitude**: Our cancer survivors maintained a positive attitude throughout and after their cancers. That doesn't mean they were always smiley and bubbly. A definably positive attitude is all about expectations, about expecting to be OK. Throughout my life and career, I've seen attitude make all the difference in the world, everywhere from the board room to the football field to the sickbed. Attitude either soothes or sabotages. It either saves or sinks. All our survivors are the happy outcomes of their personal self-fulfilling prophecies.

- **Surrounded by TRUE Supporters:** These cancer survivors knew how to find the right people to support their dreams to get well. Parents, husbands, children, siblings and friends are cited as encouraging, buoying and often promoting an against-the-odds viewpoint. In some cases, there was a cadre of supporters; in others, just one crucial person made the difference. Sometimes the person was unaware of his or her influence, as is often the case with small children. Nonetheless, the survivors in this book understood and acted on the need for the RIGHT support system.

- **Better After Than Before:** It is amazing and heart-warming to me to report that most of the survivors, who have been to hell and back, are now stronger, better and more giving as a result of their ordeals. Many say that if their journey helps even one person it was all worth it. They are true winners with a new gusto for living, learning and loving. They give meaning to their suffering and have achieved a higher level of human evolution. They connect beyond themselves to help others find self-fulfillment.

It's important to note that in virtually every case, the cancer survivors tapped MORE THAN ONE of these strategies, with the support of family and friends almost always cited as one of the keys to success.

I urge everyone reading this book to look at these common denominators. Whether you are currently in the throes of cancer or helping someone who is, you will find support from the toughest survivors. Not every story will speak directly to you, but you may find the right personal mix and, as Shakespeare said, "...grapple it to your soul with hoops of steel." For it is from these strategies and tactics that you will make your own miracle.

Don't Quit

When things go wrong, as they sometimes will,
When the road you're trudging seems all uphill,
When the funds are low and the debts are high,
And you want to smile, but you have to sigh,
When care is pressing you down a bit,
Rest if you must, but don't you quit.

Life is queer with its twists and turns,
As everyone of us sometimes learns,
And many a failure turns about
When he might have won had he stuck it out;
Don't give up, though the pace seems slow -
You might succeed with another blow.

Often the goal is nearer than
It seems to a faint and faltering man,
Often the struggler has given up
When he might have captured the victor's cup.
And he learned too late, when the night slipped down,
How close he was to the golden crown.

Success is failure turned inside out -
The silver tint of the clouds of doubt -
And you never can tell how close you are,
It may be near when it seems afar;
So stick to the fight when you're hardest hit -
It's when things seem worst that you mustn't quit.

—Unknown

"God really doesn't send you anymore than you can bear. And, to make sure, He sends you the help you need to get through it."

Bad Things Do NOT Happen To Me

Terri Bronocco Jones

I have had breast cancer. I have lost my hair. Had chemotherapy, a bone marrow transplant and been on a round trip journey to hell. Yet I remain unshaken in my belief that I have been blessed in life and bad things do not happen to me.

I'd like to share with you five survival hints that helped me come out the other side of cancer *more* confident in the goodness and fullness of life.

Hint #1:

No matter what you hear about treatments and protocols, whether it's chemo, radiation, surgery, and no matter whom you hear it from—if it didn't happen yesterday, it has been improved. The advances are nonstop.

Let me tell you something else about all the treatments. A friend said to me one day, "How awful." My reply to her was, "How wonderful." These are miracles—albeit most unpleasant—but miracles nonetheless.

Hint #2:

Never lose your sense of humor—no matter how hard it is. Norman Cousins wrote a whole book about the healing power of laughter. I watched a lot of *Nick at Night* and giggled when I realized that, without hair, you really have big ears and look like a human Chihuahua.

Not only could I laugh, I could make those who loved me laugh too. For example, I had my family and friends in stitches when I told them that, with my big ears, perhaps I was the illegitimate daughter of Ross Perot. That was especially funny to us Texans.

Hint #3:

Tell everyone you know. There was only a split second between my diagnosis and my first phone call. First of all, the more people who know the greater the likelihood of really neat presents. Most importantly, like me, you will be touched by the nonstop outpouring of encouragement and support. A dear friend of mine helped form a loose confederation of other friends we called the "possums." Possum being the Latin word for "I can." I also received hundreds of good wishes from people whose lives I must have touched in unnoticed ways but whose generosity of spirit leave me with a profound sense of humility. Joseph Conrad wrote: "The purpose of the journey is compassion," and I can assure you that's a lesson I learned early.

Hint #4:

Have faith. I'm a Roman Catholic and have an unshakeable belief in God. I took comfort in knowing there is always something more. Something greater than my sense of self. Greater than the talents and skills of the medical profession. No matter what shape YOUR faith takes, you have to believe. Sometimes in the dark of night, it's all you have to hang onto. But you get nourished and sustained without even knowing it's happening. God really doesn't send you any more than you can bear. And, to make sure, He sends you the help you need to get through it. I am reminded of the story of the man who said to God: "Why did you leave me in these terrible times? Why weren't you walking with me?" God replied: "In those times of trouble, I was not walking beside you. I carried you."

Hint #5:

Have hope. During World War II, Winston Churchill delivered one of the shortest commencement speeches on record. He said, "Never, never, never give up." I remain hopeful about my future. I once said I wanted to live just long enough for medical science to discover a cure for breast cancer. Now, I plan to live long past that. Each year I run the Susan G. Komen "Race for the Cure" with more than 15,000 women all sharing the same vision and hope. Together we will see many years pass, many babies born and all breast cancer specialists put out of work.

My odyssey reminds me of something Ralph Waldo Emerson said about us humans: "What lies behind us and what lies before us is nothing compared to what lies within us." There must be easier ways than breast cancer to discover that truth, but learning it proves what I've always said: "Bad things do NOT happen to me."

Editor's Note: Terri Bronocco Jones is Executive Director of Women Involved In Nurturing, Giving, Sharing, Inc (WINGS), a nonprofit organization dedicated to providing top-quality breast cancer care for uninsured and under-insured women in Texas. She is a recipient of the Oprah Winfrey "Use Your Life" award.

"Music was my hope…my solace…my miracle."

Scribblings

Matthew Zachary

Music is the very fabric of my soul.

Classically trained at 11, I started playing piano professionally by 16 with aspirations to become a film composer. A college senior majoring in Music, I was diagnosed at 21 with a *medullablastoma*, a rare pediatric brain cancer, the most detrimental symptom of which was the severely compromised usage of my left hand. Other symptoms were equally serious and degenerative, including severe headaches, slurring of speech, dizziness and fainting.

My first question to the neurosurgeon wasn't "Am I going to live?" It was "Am I going to play the piano again?" I was told that I would be lucky to walk, let alone ever play the piano again.

Miraculously, I survived my surgery and, indeed, I did have to retrain myself to walk, eat and swallow. However, the most important thing was to see if I could play again—<u>and I could</u>. However, the muscles in my left hand had atrophied from neuro-degenerative paralysis. [NOTE: I spent years retraining from scratch, trying to regain some of the skills and dexterity that my ten years of training had brought me—and that my cancer destroyed.]

Post-operative protocol consisted of 33 treatments of high-dose, craniospinal radiation. I experienced several serious side effects with a highly compromised quality of life. My average day consisted of 20 hours sleeping and 4 hours split up between hospital visits, uncontrollable regurgitation and playing the piano.

I decided not to let cancer destroy my art. I forced myself to play piano daily, even if it was just for ten minutes. During that time, I would "scribble" down my musical ideas on staff paper for the next time, not knowing if there would actually be a next time.

My identity had been stripped away. The only way I could identify with myself was by how much "scribbling" I did that day. Music was my hope and my only gauge for quality of life during those torturous months. My "scribblings" were my solace...my miracle.

Treatments ended. Despite the odds, I graduated from college with honors and ran a successful computer-consulting business for a few years—until I realized that my day job was getting in the way of my dream. So I quit my career to live my dream. Nine years and two best-selling solo piano CDs later (*Scribblings* and *Every Step of the Way*), I was ready to make a real difference.

Today, I am the Founder and Executive Director of Steps For Living, Inc.—a nonprofit corporation dedicated to the celebration of cancer survivorship. Our mission is to make a positive difference in the lives of newly diagnosed as well as short- and long-term cancer survivors, their families, their caregivers and those in the medical community.

My life's work is dedicated to those less fortunate than I. My message to everyone facing challenge is to be true to yourself and to stay connected to the things that bring meaning into your life. I do believe in miracles. I'm one of them.

"Life in and of itself is a miracle. We are all here for a different purpose."

The Joy of Survival

Jamie Hutchings

My story began on March 9, 1978 in the small town of Henderson, Nevada. I was off to a fresh start as a whopping 10 lb. 2 oz. baby girl. That was the beginning of my existence, but life as I know it now, didn't begin until January of 1988 when I was 9.

I had been battling "flu-like" symptoms for over two weeks and on January 12th things went from bad to worse. My mother rushed me to Urgent Care when my fever spiked to 104°F. None of us were prepared for what was to come—I was diagnosed with Acute Myelocetic Leukemia (AML), a cancer rarely found in young children. The outlook was grim my parents were told—20% chance of survival; six months to live.

The very word, "cancer" struck fear in the heart of a naïve nine-year-old. It was the equivalent of death. The only stories I'd ever heard were of people dying. "Am I going to die? What did I do to God to deserve this?" These were the only two questions that I could mutter. Of course, all my parents could say was, "You're going to be fine." But, no one could have truly prepared us for the battle ahead.

If we could find a match for a bone marrow transplant, my

chances would increase, but there were long waiting lists. Miraculously, we didn't have to look too far for a donor. My four-year-old brother, Aaron, was a perfect match. My preparation for the transplant was grueling. In order for my family to come into the room to visit me, they had to wear what we called a "space suit," covered from head to toe, with only an opening for the eyes, so as not to expose me to anything that could be transferred from the skin.

My journey was tough. Many times I wondered why I was still here. I have come to realize that life in and of itself is a miracle. We are all here for a different purposes, and if I was saved just to help give someone else hope through his or her journey, it was all worth it.

I went into remission after two-and-a-half months of treatments and, in April, I was scheduled for the bone marrow transplant. However, the doctors found a left ventricular hypertrophy in my heart and had they proceeded with the transplant, my heart would have stopped. I immediately received a heart muscle biopsy, and to everyone's delight, the condition completely reversed itself. The transplant was then put on hold. In 1988, the chances of survival beyond two years without a transplant were slim to none. I thank the Lord every night of my life that I am now 15 years past treatment and transplant free. My heart overflows with gratitude for all my blessings and the incredible support system of my parents, brother and husband that ultimately pushed me through my battles.

I am 26 and just celebrated my four-year wedding anniversary to the most wonderful man in the world. It took a great deal of courage for him to marry someone with a medical history like mine. There was a time when we thought we might never have children. But, we have been blessed with two beautiful angels that fill our lives with joy. Nikki Renee is two-and-a-half and as sweet and smart as can be. Kayli Belle just turned one-month old and is an absolute joy.

I have witnessed firsthand the joy of survival and I know without a doubt that miracles can happen to anyone who will just believe.

*"The positive thinker sees the invisible,
feels the intangible, and achieves the impossible."*

—Elbert Hubbard

"The more treatments I had, the better my mindset. It got easier…the unknown became more known."

Conquering the Unknown

Brian O'Reilly

I'm a typical teenager. I was when my cancer hit, and I am now.

When I was first diagnosed with osteogenic sarcoma, an aggressive bone cancer, my biggest fear was fear of the unknown. I was 15. Would I survive? If I did, where would I be five years from now? What would 32 weeks of intensive chemotherapy be like? Would the surgery save my left leg or would they have to amputate?

It was really scary how the lump on my leg kept growing. In just five days it went from the size of a golf ball to larger than a grapefruit. I felt like I was carrying a dumbbell in my knee. As the chemotherapy progressed, I kept getting physically weaker. Loss of weight, decreased blood counts, mouth sores and infections made me a regular at the hospital. But the more treatments I had, the better my mindset. It got easier…the unknown become more known.

The pivotal day for me was the day of my limb-sparing surgery. Thankfully, the leg didn't have to be amputated. Instead, they replaced my femur and knee with a metal prosthesis. After the surgery, I became totally determined to get better. I knew I could finish the rest of the chemo, regardless of how sick I felt.

I'll never forget May 24th, 2000. It was the last day I spent in the hospital. Five surgeries, ten months of chemotherapy, over 160 days in the hospital and a year's worth of bone scans and cat scans. OVER. I missed my entire junior year of high school, but crammed just about a year's worth of work into a few weeks and passed all my finals. I didn't mind studying. I was just happy to be walking around without an IV pole. I had a new appreciation for living and learned that priorities I had before are not as important when you're fighting to survive. And I had the best ending. Thanks to the Make-A-Wish Foundation, I got to go to the Sydney Olympics.

I'm 18 now and a sophomore at Cornell. I'm happy I only have to get checked out twice a year and my prosthesis is holding up OK, except for the occasional mishaps with airport metal detectors. If that's the only problem I've got to deal with, I'll take it. I'm a teenager again. Just a little less cocky and ten times more resilient.

"My '3P' philosophy became my personal ammunition of attitude for fighting cancer: Physician, Positive Attitude, Prayer."

The 3Ps

Mike Panther

First, I was shocked. Then I was scared. Then I was angry. Then I resolved to beat this thing called cancer.

After having gone through a lot of emotions, I developed my 3P philosophy, which became my personal ammunition of attitude for fighting cancer:

Physician—I would get the best advice I could find, consider treatment options, pick one and go for it.

Positive Attitude—I had done some reading about cancer patients and found a common theme of success resulting from this attitude. Switching from my initial reactions of anger and fear wasn't too hard for me since I am basically an optimistic person.

Prayer—I turned to God for strength and I turned to family and friends for their prayer support.

My 3Ps came largely out of my not being ready for the scathing diagnosis I received from my dermatologist. "Mr. Panther," he said, "you have malignant melanoma. This is a life-threatening disease. If there are things you always wanted to do and have never done, I suggest you do them now." Thankfully, my wife was in the treatment room with me to hear the same words and stay focused on the next steps the doctor recommended. For me, the conversation between them was surreal, something of a dream. I heard that a second surgery was going to be needed. I heard names of possible physicians to contact being discussed. I heard that whatever route I chose there would be serious decisions to be made. I was petrified and I was getting angry, with my anger aimed at a lot of targets.

First, there was this dermatologist. How dare he be so uncaring…so callous. Bedside manner sure wasn't in his vocabulary. Next was God. How could He let this happen to me? How could He let this impact so negatively my family, the people I cared about most? I wanted to grow old gracefully with my wife; see our children become productive adults; see our grandchildren come into this world; and do so much more.

Then it became clear to me that I needed to get past fear and anger to a better attitude and so I made the shift to the 3P philosophy. We scheduled the next surgery and began looking into post-operative treatment options. About six months after my initial diagnosis, my oncologist told me I was cancer free. I remember sitting up and yelling a loud: "YES!"

I am now eight years cancer free. I have regular exams. I stay positive. I pray daily for health and for those who remembered me in their prayers. The "busy-ness" of life still works hard to divert my focus from the important things, but the 3Ps work equally hard to keep me attentive to the right things.

"So make the best of this test...hang it on a shelf in good health and good time."

Make the Best of This Test

Laurice Strausser

My personal experience with cancer began when I was 27 years old, just eight weeks after my first daughter was born. My diagnosis was Ewing sarcoma, a form of bone cancer. Prior to my diagnosis, I had suffered from what we thought was tendonitis. During my pregnancy, the so-called tendonitis got worse and worse and after my daughter was born, the pain became unbearable. A bone scan and MRI revealed the cancer.

My treatment consisted of four rounds of chemotherapy; then surgery; then four more rounds of chemotherapy. When my hair began to fall out, I decided to have it shaved rather than endure the slow clump-by-clump process. I remember how traumatic it was standing in front of my husband for the first time completely bald. What a help it was when he hugged me and told me how beautiful I was.

My daughter was only a few months old when I was going through my illness. Needless to say she needed a lot of care. I wasn't the one who was the primary caregiver. It was my mother. I thanked God for her tireless help and I thank God for her today every time I look back. She also did some other amazing things which helped support and heal me. For example, she hired a dietician, a woman who was a cancer survivor herself, and who felt nutritional supplements were vital to recovery and maintained remission. She gave me a list of 16 supplements to take daily. I did; and I too believe they were vital to my recovery. Although I did go through the nausea and weakness with the chemo, I seemed to bounce back quickly.

After the four months of chemo, it was time for my surgery, called radical resection of the left humerus. The cancerous bone was removed and replaced with a prosthesis. After the surgery, we were told 100% nacrosis—YEAH!!!! I had four more rounds of chemo to go and I gladly took them. I would do anything to keep the cancer away.

I read books, meditated, had two Reiki sessions with a master, changed my diet, continued with the supplements along with Essiac tea and I prayed. We also started a tradition. I wore, as did all those who were close to me, an angel on the left shoulder—the one that had had the cancer.

I now have two daughters and am cancer free. There is a great song by Greenday which has some lines I find especially helpful as I look back—and forward:

...So make the best of this test and don't ask why
It's not a question, but a lesson learned in time...
So take the photographs and still frames in your mind
Hang it on a shelf in good health and good time
Tattoos and memories and asking on trial
For what it's worth it was worth all the while
It's something unpredictable, but in the end is right
I hope you have the time of your life.

"Slowly but surely, I began to realize that I did not want to die! I would NOT accept my prognosis."

Hope is There for the Taking

Jana Brabec

Do you believe in miracles? Well, I do.

Twenty-one years ago I overcame malignant melanoma, only to be stricken with stage IV breast cancer. My doctors gave me a 5% chance of surviving two years.

I calmly called my daughter, Kim, and filled her in on the situation. The next thing I knew, she joined me and remained with me throughout my long ordeal. Then reality hit me. I could not think or function. Everything seemed to be in slow motion. Thank God Kim was with me.

After living through a few weeks like a zombie, things started to take focus. The blurred images were beginning to sharpen and take shape. Slowly but surely, I began to realize that I did not want to die! I would NOT accept my prognosis. With my daughter's help and support, I began to organize a path toward recovery. We listened to my doctors and asked a lot of questions. We spent endless hours researching my disease. Remember, 21 years ago there was no Internet—we had to do it the old-fashioned way.

As my body began down a very medicated path in an attempt to heal, I realized that my mind and my spirit needed healing as well. They needed to help my body through its ordeal. The protocol of treatments, chemo, surgery and radiation would take their toll.

Although I had a strong faith, I knew I had to strengthen my bond with God. I prayed and prayed. My prayers were answered. God sent me an angel and it was my daughter, Kim.

In our research, Kim and I also began to understand how important it was that I not catch anything. The powerful chemo had reduced my immune system to practically nothing. A simple cold could literally kill me! With the help of a master formulator, I began a vitamin and herbal regimen. Throughout my over two-year-long chemo-filled battle, I did not catch a cold, and I had no viral or bacterial infections. (I also practiced visualization techniques in which I pictured the chemo running through my body, enveloping and destroying any and every cancer cell.)

That in itself was a miracle! But there's more.

During my first three months of chemo, I could actually feel the tumor shrinking. A mastectomy followed with a pathology report stating "only microscopic evidence found in the breast tissue." Another miracle, I had had an 6cm tumor and it was gone!

What was it that accounted for my dramatic success that defied 95% odds? Was it the finest physicians? My positive attitude? My vitamins? Divine intervention? I know God had his hand on my shoulder and still does.

I can tell you that to this day I continue to practice my deep faith, strive to maintain a positive attitude and take my anti-oxidant formula. I remain healthy and illness free and know I was spared for a reason. Today, through my company and my foundation, my anti-oxidant formula helps countless others.

By sharing my story, I want to bring hope to anyone who is facing what seem to be insurmountable odds. In hope you will find the will and the courage to fight, to survive and to share the precious gift of life.

"Believe that healing is meant for you!"

Twelve Years Later and Feeling Great

Tami Salinas

I was 27 years old with no past medical history and in the hospital for a relatively routine and elective back surgery. This was not supposed to happen. On the day I was to be discharged I woke with severe abdominal pains. It turned out to be stage IV cancer with a mass in my chest the size of a grapefruit and bone marrow involvement.

Because of the advanced stage of my cancer, I wound up staying in the hospital for six more weeks. When I was able to go home, I was forty pounds lighter, bald and unable to walk up the two steps to get into our house. Chemotherapy continued for six months.

The incredible part of my story is that I was also a new Christian and had the faith of a child. I was never afraid. Through high fevers, low white blood cell counts and endless hours of vomiting, my faith allowed me to keep smiling. My attitude was: "If I live, I win. If I die, I win." Looking back, only God could have given me that peace.

After the completion of the chemo, things were going well and life was returning to normal except that the chemo had caused my ovaries to stop functioning and the doctor told me it would be highly unlikely I would ever have another child. That was OK since I already had two beautiful boys. Because of my youngish age, the doctor had me start taking hormones to promote ovulation. One night I went to a healing service at our church and decided I wanted everything back to normal. I went forward and explained to the pastor that I had been healed of cancer, but that my ovaries were non-functional and I would like to be 100%.

During my next ultrasound, my gynecologist saw a spot on my ovary. Everyone panicked. They decided to wait and see what happened. The next month the cyst was even larger and it looked amazingly like an ovulating cyst, which was highly unlikely. He said I could go off the hormone and see what happened. Well what happened is I got pregnant. Yes, that's right. God blessed me with a baby. I was nervous though because it had been six months exactly from finishing chemo that I got pregnant, and that's the very soonest recommended.

Well, I had an incredible pregnancy. I felt great and after two very long and difficult deliveries with my other boys, our third son was born within two hours of our getting to the hospital. What a miracle.

There is life—lots of it—after cancer. I am now a 12-year survivor. My boys are 19, 18 and 10. I work full-time as a nurse. I enjoy many activities with family and friends and life is truly wonderful. My message to you is have faith and believe that healing is meant for you.

"Brent has made it against all odds.
Because of him, our family realizes how blessed we are
to have one another."

One of a Kind: Brent Barringer

by Chad Barringer

I am writing to share a story of survival, courage and hope. My brother, Brent, was diagnosed with a malignant brain cancer in 1976 at the age of four. I was six months old at the time. All our lives changed dramatically within days that summer. Everything happened so quickly. Brent's symptoms included loss of balance, nose bleeds and uncontrolled vomiting. His pediatrician recognized that Brent might have a brain tumor and immediately referred him to a specialist. After various tests and CT scans, Brent was indeed found to have a large malignant tumor on his brain stem.

Within a week, Brent had surgery and the tumor was removed. Following surgery, he went into a coma for three months, was tube fed and given radiation treatments. My parents were told he had only a 25% chance of survival. Brent managed to emerge from the coma, but his mental and physical capacities were impaired by the surgery and treatments. He came home just days before his fifth birthday. He was both the same child and a different child. He could still laugh and play like the old Brent, but learning was now a major challenge and he lacked normal coordination and development.

Brent spent most of his early years in special needs schools. As he got older, one of his dreams was to be able to attend high school just like everyone else. With the help of teachers and counselors he was able to do that at 16. Although in learning disabled programs, he was now able to attend art and physical education classes with the other students. He even decided to be a sports manager, and at some point, he was the manager for every sport his high school offered. After four years, Brent walked across the stage and received a certificate that he had attended high school.

My parents weren't sure what would happen after high school. Through a county program, he got a job washing dishes, and although he disliked it, he stuck with it for a few years. He eventually got a job doing maintenance work and several years ago he was asked to help out on a small, family-run poultry farm. He loves the job and the family says Brent is a great help in keeping their farm operating and that they could not do it without him.

Despite all Brent's struggles and hardships, he is one of the kindest and most loving individuals I know. He always thinks about others before himself. He has made our family realize how important each day is and how blessed we are to have one another. Brent is an inspiration to all those around him and a true "one of a kind." Against all odds, he is 33 and doing well.

"Cancer kickstarted my life...and what an incredible life it has become."

"And the Winner Is...Greg Fornelli!"

Greg Fornelli

What were you doing in 1995? I was fighting for my life, day by day. You might think I would look back on those days with horror. But oddly, that's really not the case. Let me tell you why.

Fast forward to September 2002. I'm the president of my own thriving little company named Stock Car Steel & Aluminum. I'm in an audience of business and professional people in Charlotte, North Carolina, as the master of ceremonies announces the recipient of the Charlotte Chamber of Commerce Entrepreneur of the Year Award.

"And the winner is...Greg Fornelli!"

I hear the applause. And it's for me. Who would believe this? How could I tell these people that in some strange, miraculous way I owed this award to the cancer diagnosis I received just a few years earlier? But you can say that diagnosis actually kicked started my life—and what an incredible life it has become.

Back to 1995. I was 30 years old and married to my college sweetheart, Deborah. Our daughter Hayley was just one month old when I began suffering numbness in my face. My family doctor didn't have any answers. We thought it might just pass. Months later, it had not passed. An MRI provided no clues. Eye problems led me to an optometrist but not to any insights. It was a toothache that took me to a dentist, who made at last the fateful discovery through some x-rays.

The diagnosis: an extremely rare type of jaw bone cancer. The prognosis: a less than 17 percent chance of survival. The numbness in my face was nothing compared to the numbness I felt at the core of my soul.

My journey against the odds took me to Memorial Sloan-Kettering Cancer Center in New York City. They were fabulous. But I learned through this ordeal that healing is about much more than medical treatment. A close friend and I used to relate friendship to a bank account, you know, where you're continually making deposits and withdrawals. I had to make plenty of "withdrawals" during that hard, hard time.

I also made plenty of trips to the side of the crib where my daughter, Hayley, lay sleeping. There in those silent moments I entered that state of mind where a promise and a prayer become kind of the same thing. You know what I'm talking about, don't you? I promised her that I would walk her down the aisle on the day of her wedding. Yes, I'd be there for her.

In fact, I never stopped planning for the future. That's a major ingredient to keeping hopeful. I knew I wanted to start a business that would supply metals to NASCAR teams. I knew its potential and I knew it would work. There was no way cancer was going to get in the way of that dream.

But I needed help. Lots of it. And everywhere I turned it seemed to be there waiting for me. How did I make it through this? I'll boil it down to three things.

Love. There's no greater power.

Hope. It makes you plan for the future.

Determination. When it comes to your life, don't ever take *no* for an answer.

I truly believe I am alive today because of the love I felt around me. My life has become a series of one incredible occurrence after another, far beyond anything I ever envisioned, growing up back in Kansas. Now every morning, thanks to all that love, I hear the echo of those words in my heart: "*And the winner is...* ***Greg Fornelli!***" Oh, yes. That is so true.

"Ingenuity, plus courage, plus work, equals miracles."

—Bob Richards

"Miracles come in small steps and
you have to work for them.
Dig deep and bring them out in your life.
Cancer CAN be beaten. Never give up."

Blessed

Paul Leverett

When I was diagnosed with the worst kind of brain cancer, Stage IV brain stem glioblastoma multiforme, I was marketing manager for the oil well drilling division of a major conglomerate and living in Jakarta. In my business, we were forced to figure out how to put drilling rigs to work in conditions they were never designed for. Our attitude to a customer's requirement? Can do.

That was the attitude I took into my battle with this supposed death-sentence cancer—a cancer that the experts predicted left me with at most a year to live and less than a 1% chance of long-term survival. I was treated in Houston because that was home to some of the best doctors in the field. None of them held out any hope, so I had to create my own kind of hope.

I could not, would not take dying this way. My kind of tumor doubles in size every two weeks. It was like something out of the Sigourny Weaver "Alien" movies, and I needed help outside myself to reverse it. I did not want to die. I was in love. I wanted to live. One night, I went to our bedroom and got on my knees and started praying to God. I had not prayed in 25 years. I begged the

Lord to guide me. Give me peace. Heal me. I needed a miracle.

I began to feel things were happening in my life which were the work of the Holy Spirit. My wife, Jennie, and my friends, my company, my insurance—everyone was backing me. No financial worries since the company was paying; all kinds of support because friends and family were praying. One brought me holy water from Lourdes. Another just grabbed my head and cursed the tumor, telling it to leave his friend alone.

Nothing conventional was working, so I decided to try the controversial Dr. Burzynski approach of antineoplastons, which my wife Jennie and I learned to administer through an inserted catheter. The MRI after 12 weeks on the treatment indicated a more than 10% reduction in the tumor. Good news. Continue. A little more than five months after starting the antineoplastons, the tumor was reduced by approximately 75%. The following December, I was declared in complete remission. In September 2001, I stopped the Burzynski treatments.

Can you believe it? No hope of making it out of 1999 alive and yet we killed the tumor.

I've been told I'm a walking miracle. I know I am. Miracles come in small steps. If you want a miracle, I believe you have to work for it. Believe in miracles. Pray. Have faith. Meditate. Repeat affirmations. Do whatever you need to do to survive. Study and apply yourself. God lives in each and every one of us. Dig deep and bring this out in your life. Always remember cancer can be beaten. Never give up.

"A good attitude can go a long way.
God has tested me and so far I'm passing."

A Coach's Attitude

Kevin Klug

I have always loved playing sports. My true passion was soccer. Coaching my son as he grew up gave me a lot of personal satisfaction. I did it until I started having seizures. My wife told me I shouldn't continue and, reluctantly, I agreed. I didn't want to embarrass him or myself, so I quit coaching.

But let me back up a bit.

Playing in the yard one day, a sharp pain cut right through my abdomen. I shrugged it off, knowing I had played 80 minutes of soccer the day before. I had terrible cramps in the same area after that until the night I had my first grand mal seizure. I fell out of bed, cutting my head on the night stand. By the time I arrived at the hospital, I was trying to figure out what happened.

More seizures followed as my wife and I saw a number of oncologists. Finally, a surgeon gave it to me point blank. "You have a brain tumor." I had my first craniotomy in early 1991. My second operation was a year later in 1992 and I was diagnosed as GMB IV. I won't go into a lot of medical details, mainly because I either don't know what happened or can't remember. I have been plagued with migraine headaches all my life.

At some point during the radiation treatments following the second operation I asked the doctor how many more treatments were left from the original 35. When she came back with a pocket calculator and sent me back to the simulator, it hit me and hit me hard: "You idiot, this is serious!" But, having lost a daughter to a congenital heart defect, I knew nothing could be worse and that I could cope with whatever was going to happen.

Following the radiation, I underwent a variety of chemos for about six months; but the tumor kept growing wildly and the doctor told my wife I had three to six months to live. It was at that time that I was accepted into the first human gene therapy study for glioblastoma brain tumors. It meant two more operations—one for the injections and one to stop the hemorrhaging that followed. During the second surgery, I wound up in a coma with partial paralysis on my left side. Now, it's more than ten years later and I have no signs of any tumor growth.

It was all worth it because it gave me a chance to see my children grow up. I cannot do the things that once came so easy, but I believe it is God's way of testing me. So far I'm passing. A good attitude can go a long way.

"I emailed, snail mailed and phoned everyone who'd want to know and asked for prayers and encouragement. I was rewarded tenfold."

A Different Outcome

Kathryn Phenix

In my 14 years as a hospice nurse, I had always marveled at my patients' courage. I often questioned if I could go through what they did. I found it only took three words to cement my resolve and make me fight: "YOU HAVE CANCER."

Let me clarify why the breast cancer diagnosis was especially tough for me and my husband. In my 31 years as a nurse, all the breast cancer patients I took care of died. My husband's first wife battled breast cancer for 4 years. I met them when I had to admit her to our hospice home care program and she died within three months of her admission. Six months later Paul invited me over for a cup of coffee and a piece of chocolate cake which he had baked himself. Our first date was March 1st and we were engaged on March 27th.

Twelve-and-a-half years later, I had no idea how I was going to tell Paul I had a lump in my breast. After the sonogram, I drove to his office. From the parking lot I could tell he was busy with his staff, so I went home. Unfortunately, his secretary had seen me. He called shortly after I got home and asked, "What's up?" I told him about the lump and he was home in five minutes. We just held each other and cried. We both had so much bad history with this disease.

The biopsy confirmed our worst fears—this was a cancerous growth. The good news? No lymph node involvement. The bad news? My borders were not free of cancer and I would require a mastectomy. With a second opinion and studies of my right breast we decided on bilateral mastectomies, chemo and radiation. I would do anything to keep it at bay.

I emailed, snail mailed and phoned everyone who'd want to know and asked for prayers and encouragement. I was rewarded tenfold with daily cards, letters and emails. My husband was initially reluctant about my getting the word out, because his first wife had been very private about the disease. When he saw the response, he admitted he was wrong. It was the only "wrong" thing he did. Every night he'd draw a bubble bath for me followed by a full body massage. He cleaned, cooked and shopped. I never feared cancer would come between us and I was right.

I am now a four-year survivor of Stage II B breast cancer. My faith is much stronger, and it, combined with the love of family and friends, sees me through. I feel strongly that I must give back and help educate women to act quickly if they find something out-of-the-ordinary. I teach classes in breast health and am also a Reach to Recovery volunteer. As both a nurse and cancer survivor, I am confident we will soon see the day when women don't have to be fearful if they feel a lump.

"Live in love and light. Life is a celebration!"

Rebel WITH a Cause

Linda Kedy

I guess I've always been a bit of a rebel. After I was diagnosed with breast cancer, my antennae went up when doctor after doctor insisted I immediately have a radical bilateral mastectomy. My intuition kept telling me not to, but it was difficult because I had no family or local support to consult with and discuss alternatives.

I went to Palm Springs, California to work with healer friends and begin the emotional work of ridding myself of the guilt surrounding my body and my family relationships. Once back home in Atlanta, I realized I had to let go of my daughter, whom I had been trying to help overcome a drug addiction. We arranged for her to move back with family overseas; and today both she and I are so much healthier as a result of this period of separation.

A friend referred me to Dr. Geffen, who wrote *The Journey Through Cancer.* He was an absolute blessing; consulting with me over the phone; and putting me in touch with a plastic surgeon for natural reconstruction (using my tummy to rebuild my breasts.) All the while, my local surgeons were against this procedure claiming it would leave me with no abdominal muscles. Wrong! I wound up choosing the natural reconstruction surgeon with the highest recommendations.

In preparation for this massive intrusion to my body (five hours of surgery in which I would be cut wide with about 50 inches of incisions), I went to a Chinese herbologist and began a regimented routine to cleanse and strengthen my body. For the surgery itself, I asked for the absolute minimum of drugs and put myself into a meditative state with great CD music. When I woke up, I had them immediately remove the morphine drip.

Once released from the hospital, if I had listened to the doctors, I would have stayed home for weeks with minimal activity. The cancer was out. I was cleared emotionally. I began a strict regimen of taking care of myself following my own intuition to strengthen and heal. At 9 days, I had sex—carefully. At 3 weeks I went Salsa dancing—carefully—and climbed Stone Mountain—slowly. At 4 weeks, against doctors' orders, I flew to Hawaii to visit with my son for a month. What better place to recuperate?

When I returned, my doctor told me I looked amazingly well and asked, "What have you been doing?" I grinned. "Not seeing you." Since I don't do drugs of any sort, I refused any of the protocols including chemo, radiation and tamoxifen. I continued to avoid the pollutants and carcinogens in the foods we eat and to pay attention to my emotional and spiritual needs…AND…I had my most successful year in sales while going through all this.

My advice to anyone: free up your time to do the things you love; do them today and engage your body in the youthing process to ensure health and longevity! My website, www.healThyspirits.com, shows how to live in love and light, with or without cancer. Life is a celebration!

"Would I let cancer rule my life…or…would I move on, reach out and journey forward? I decided to move on."

Ain't Life Great?

Peter DeBona

I had just met my wife to be and we were very happy. Cancer was the farthest thing from our minds. Her first husband had died from cancer and it seemed unlikely it would strike twice in a row. To our great disappointment it did. In April of 1994, I was diagnosed with glioblastoma multiforme IV, the most deadly and aggressive brain tumor of all.

With a prognosis of 4 to 6 months and the chance that the surgery could leave me with serious impediments, I needed time to put my affairs in order. So I negotiated a week from the surgeon. In that time, believe it or not, I got all my personal and financial affairs in order. We got married, complete with rings and a reception for 60 people, AND I acted as the best man at my son's wedding.

Then the inevitable: the surgery. When I woke up and realized I was alive, I began to cry. I had not thought I would ever wake up again. I subsequently underwent a series of difficult therapies, including radiation and chemo for close to a year. But, I was STILL alive.

It's important to understand that the type of cancer I have

never goes away. It almost always comes back. So I had to make a choice. Would I let it rule my life or would I move on, reach out and journey forward? I decided to move on and more than 10 years since my six-months-to-live diagnosis, I am very alive and very well and have celebrated my 61st birthday. I am even at the point now, where I can actually schedule my own MRIs. I was formerly so full of dread of a tumor being detected that I'd have my wife make the appointment and not tell me until the actual day, so I could limit my anxiety to the least amount of time.

There are so many things that have contributed to my survival: prayer, support from family and friends, volunteering, faith in God and knowing HE is the reason I am here. My life is full and cancer is only a small part of it. I have four grandchildren, including my namesake, Peter. I dedicate large portions of my time to helping others, which is really helping me. I man the Brain Tumor Hot Line for the Brain Tumor Society and the National Brain Tumor Foundation; I volunteer at my hospital's cancer center; I am a support person for the Cancer Hope Network; and I also communicate with many cancer patients through email.

I have learned how to live with this tumor and not worry about it every day. I have found my niche in life—and it is continually expanding. For example, I am getting into some great fishing with a friend and that hobby is adding a whole new dimension to my life. All I can say is, "Ain't life great?"

"Just when I found the meaning of life, they changed it."

—George Carlin

"I realized the benefit of my experience; my aloneness made me strong.
What we at first see as loss can be a postponed gain."

Taboo No More

Mona Kamel

In the area of the world where I live, Egypt, breast cancer is considered taboo. People hide it and most of the time a woman who has lost a breast is ashamed to admit it. Surprisingly, sexual function is thought to be related to the breasts. So you can understand my horror when at the age of 30 I was diagnosed with breast cancer and had to have my left breast removed along with 16 lymph nodes. Suddenly I was subject not only to terror, but also to shame. I could never face others with my scar.

The lonely nights in the hospital following the surgery were the worst for me as I faced my mutilation as well as the prospect of chemotherapy for six weeks. I could not look into a mirror. I was running into a maze of horror. I wanted to escape the nightmare...but where to go? The weird reaction of my husband, who was working in the Gulf, made things even tougher on me. He never showed up and only contacted me by phone every now and then to wish me good luck. It was obvious he couldn't face the danger, so he left me to battle alone.

It was during those long lonely nights that I discovered my inner power. Here I was all by myself harshly put off the track of my life.

Should I keep lying underground or should I stand up on my own? I wanted to see my two kids grow up; so I decided to make that wish come true by believing in the power of my own body. It had betrayed me once, but this time I was going to guide it to survival.

While dealing with the effects of chemo, I was trying to find reasons to survive. I engaged in charitable activities and social work, especially with the children and orphans of cancer patients. The more I saw of other cases, the more I was grateful about my own case. It seems that you only discover the real size of your own pain when you see the huge problems of others.

With chemo sessions ending, I could feel the power inside me growing. I almost admired the resistance of my weak body. It gave me confidence because if I could tolerate this pain, then I could do anything. A feeling of happiness replaced the bitterness I used to feel because my husband was not by my side. I then realized the benefit of my experience; my aloneness made me strong. So even what we see as loss can be a postponed gain.

To combat the ignorance and shame surrounding breast cancer in this part of the world, I have decided to help other women get information about this disease so they can find their cancer earlier. I also give support to women already diagnosed to reduce their suffering and open new horizons for them. For me, my lack of knowledge made the effects of the disease worse. As they say, the unknown is always feared. I hope I can spare others that fear.

Today, I am proudly seeing myself in the eyes of others: the dream for any woman diagnosed with breast cancer: healthy, active, and successful. And guess what? My new life style has enhanced my appearance. I am finally capable of facing the world as my scar is no longer a taboo.

"I would gladly go back to never having had breast cancer—but only if I could still be the person I have become as a result of it."

It's All About Living

Vicki Tosher

Even before breast cancer, I never played golf. Never liked it that much. Needless to say finding a lump in one's breast the size of a golf ball does nothing to make you more favorably disposed to the game. That was in May of 1992. It seems like a lifetime ago, and in some respects it was.

The diagnosis following the mastectomy: Stage III invasive ductal carcinoma of the breast. I chose an aggressive post-operative treatment which increased my chance of disease-free survival to 75% in three to five years. And here I am over 10 years later.

Breast cancer has done incredible things to me and for me. Without it I would have two breasts and still smoke two packs a day. With it I have one breast, cleaner lungs and the ability to run races and climb mountains—literally. Without it, I would have a fear of dying. With it, I am not afraid of dying (or of living for that matter).

Without cancer I would still be worrying about lots of inconsequential things and spending weekends doing chores and errands. With it, the house is a mess and for the most part, I'm happier for it. Without cancer, I would never have come to know the strength of the bonds of love. With it, those bonds have been tested and have survived, sometimes frayed, but strong, nonetheless.

Without breast cancer, I would never have met an amazing array of remarkable women. Most are still with me in life. Some have passed on, but are still with me. Those who are gone have taught me about living while dying and all have taught me about living. They have enriched my life, helped to keep me safe and helped me heal. They have been the gifts of this damned disease. I would gladly go back to never having had breast cancer—but only if I could still be the person these folks have helped me to become.

Oh, yes and there's the amazing Polly Letofsky with whom I have walked in California, New Zealand and Australia to help raise money and awareness to combat breast cancer. I have also founded and now serve as President of the Board of a unique non-profit in Colorado called Sense of Security. We provide non-medical financial assistance to breast cancer patients while they are in treatment. It helps cover housing, food and groceries, utilities, transportation, child care and health insurance premiums. Our website is: http://www.senseofsecurity.org.

As for golf? I still don't play the game, but I have become much more enamored of it since meeting some wonderful women who are avid players and who have been fantastic supporters of Sense of Security. I'm also always ready and willing to chat with anyone who has been diagnosed with breast cancer.

Editor's note: Since this was written, Vicki was diagnosed with a second primary breast cancer, had a second mastectomy and reconstructive surgery. She is pleased with her decision.

"The two things that kept me going can work for anyone.
Be confident about your protocol.
Keep your body strong."

Totally Prepared

Dr. Michael Retsky

As I think about that time, I was probably the most prepared person in the world to become a cancer patient. I had been doing breast cancer research since 1982 and especially pertinent was my research into how tumors grow. According to my theory, tumors grew in an erratic fashion, growing for a time and then becoming dormant—not in a continuous manner with gradual slowing as the current thinking held. If I were right, chemotherapy should be spread over a long time rather than just the first few months after surgery, as is more commonly done.

I had the chance to put my theory to the most personal of tests when my post colon-cancer surgery work-ups showed I was among those who suffered from the biggest danger of colon cancer—potential liver metastases. I determined there was an 80% chance of developing liver metastases without chemotherapy and a 60% with it. Those were not good odds.

Using my theory of erratic growth, I estimated the time needed for the therapy to fully cure me was about 28 months. In fact, I wound up staying on the therapy for a bit longer, two-and-a-half years. My protocol was a low dose-continuous infusion of an old colon cancer drug: 5-flourouracil. No one had before used it in the early stages of the disease. As a result of my protocol—starting when I went to sleep and running for the next six hours through a subcutaneous chemotherapy port below my right collarbone—I experienced very mild toxicity. What's more, I greatly preserved my quality of life. The pump was completely disconnected during the day and that made a world of difference psychologically. For example, I didn't have to worry about the pump making noises when I was in a movie theatre and I could exercise without having to wear it.

What kept me most hopeful was belief in the correctness of my approach and taking good care of my body. I was confident the science was right. With conventional high dose injection chemotherapy, the drug has a half-life of less than a half hour in the body. The same drug, my way, a low dose for 6 hours, had to be better. I also considered rigorous exercise to be part of the therapy. In fact, it continues to be an important part of my life. Cancer patients face high risks of surgery. The best thing I could do was keep my body strong so recovery after surgery would be rapid.

It's been nine years since the surgery and I've been off therapy for six years. All markers and scans have remained negative for cancer and I have felt fine the entire time. As a cancer researcher, I certainly was more prepared than the average cancer patient. But the two things that kept me going can work for anyone. Be confident about—and involved with—your protocol. Keep your body strong.

"My soul received a healing imprint which spoke in a resounding voice: 'If you only have faith, you will be all right. YOU WILL BE ALRIGHT!'"

Freedom

David Bradley

In a way, it's kind of ironic. My personal struggle for freedom began on Independence Day. My wife and I were enjoying the wide-eyed amazement of our two-year-old twin daughters who had just seen their first fireworks display. As we headed to the car, I started experiencing flu-like symptoms, which persisted on and off with an accompanying high fever for the next four days.

I was checked into the hospital to get the fever down and run some tests. The doctors initially suspected appendicitis or diverticulitis and determined the next logical step to be exploratory surgery.

I cannot imagine my wife's shock, pain and horror when our physician friend delivered the crushing news. "David has cancer and it's serious." I remember vividly my own reaction. I woke up in the recovery room to my wife's voice. She told me what the doctor had found. A tumor on the large intestine had perforated the intestinal wall and attached itself to my appendix and my small intestine and was invading my bladder. They removed all the cancer they could find, as well as ten lymph nodes to gauge the severity of the illness. It was very severe—stage IV of non-Hodgkin's lymphoma.

Then it all changed. I can't tell you how. How do you describe a spiritual transformation to hope? How do you describe a life-altering blessing? There are no words to explain it. My soul received a healing imprint which spoke in a resounding voice that married with my own. "If you only have faith, you will be alright. YOU WILL BE ALRIGHT!" It seems strange, even to me, that my greatest moment of freedom began with my aggressive battle against cancer. When I was released two days later and riding home with my wife and daughters, the blessings of life once again popped out at me, the blessings in the car and the blessings of God's beautiful world outside. Never before in my 35 years was it so breathtakingly clear. I cried harder than I can ever remember.

I underwent chemotherapy at the National Institute of Health in Bethesda, Maryland. Once again we were showered with blessings. My college roommate and his wife opened their home to our entire family one week out of three for the next five months, allowing us the joy of all being together. My wife showed amazing strength and shouldered unimaginable responsibilities. Our friends were all eager to help and she, knowing the value of their involvement to both them and us, assigned them tasks. This approach created a community of love that brilliantly broke down the walls of isolation so often felt by cancer patients and those who care about them.

I have had a clean bill of health for six years. I breathe deeper of life than ever and see blessings everywhere. My faith, my family, my friendships are all stronger as a result of my cancer. To God be the glory.

"Where there is love there are always miracles."

—Willa Cather

"In my mind, I 'blasted' every cancer cell with the force of Luke Skywalker battling Darth Vader."

Pregnant With Hope

Stacey Polak

Suddenly, out of nowhere, I had a 50% chance of survival and the baby in my womb had none. I was diagnosed with non-Hodgkin's lymphoma at the age of 29 while 12 weeks pregnant. How could this happen to a young, non-smoking vegetarian who tried to do everything right?

Then I found my oncologist, my hero. He made it clear that he wasn't going to let me die and he found research to indicate CHOP chemotherapy, given during the second trimester, would cause only "transient" problems to the baby—problems which could be treated. We decided to continue the pregnancy and monitor with high-tech ultrasounds to watch for signs of trouble. The chemo, combined with the pregnancy, created the worst symptoms imaginable. I lost 25 pounds because mouth and throat sores made it impossible for me to chew and swallow. I forced myself to sip juice and special shakes for my baby, despite the pain. I was dizzy, could barely walk, and sometimes would throw up as much as 20 times a day. My body hurt to the point where I could no longer avoid morphine. Yes, my body was devastated; but my spirit never wavered. I had to survive for the baby in my womb and my two-year-old son. My children needed me and I couldn't conceive of missing their growing up.

It was worth it. The chemo worked. Immediately, the tumor started shrinking and I began a routine of meditation, rest and guided imagery. In my mind, I "blasted" every cancer cell with the force of Luke Skywalker battling Darth Vader. My oncologist gave me reassurance and hope and most of all, my parents gave me encouragement, strength and emotional support. They were my energy and optimism when fear raised its ugly voice.

I went into labor five-and-a-half weeks early. Twelve hours later my healthy, gorgeous, prizefighter daughter, Shayna Ruth, was born. She showed no bad effects from the chemo and even had a full head of hair. My "huge" tumor shrunk to the size of a pea. When I began my 20 radiation treatments to clean up the area of last cancer cells, I had a full head of curly short hair and was ready to begin living again.

Now I am living my dreams and meeting my goals as a contented, complete, single, working mom. I speak to cancer patients at my hospital whenever asked. When I see someone on chemo, I introduce myself as a survivor and show them my long, thick, beautifully curly hair and let them know chemo once took every last hair on my head, too! I love to see them smile and feel the power which hope can inspire!

"I understand as a Christian, I was not promised I would never have problems, but I was promised that He would never leave or forsake me. This assurance was the only way I could have made it through my cancer battle."

"Praise God From Whom All Blessings Flow"

Tony Presley

Fourteen years ago, I thought I was one of the healthiest people in Georgia. I ran. I was a high school coach. I ate healthy. Then, at 42, I was diagnosed with non-Hodgkin's lymphoma. The problem started with back pain which kept getting worse and worse. The usual muscle relaxants brought no relief.

One morning as I was shaving I discovered an alarming lump around the size of a goose egg between my neck and my collarbone. A biopsy revealed it was non-Hodgkin's lymphoma, a form of cancer I knew little about. I was about to find out more than I wanted to know…first hand. CAT scans showed my lymphoma was fairly advanced and had affected a large cluster of lymph nodes in my abdominal area. That's what was causing the backaches.

One of the toughest parts was telling my family. My wife was a strong and loving pillar of support. My parents, my brothers and their families were always there and more than willing to do anything and everything to help. I drew much of my strength from their prayers, the prayers of my Church family and the extended Christian family. Early on, I turned the situation over to God, who had sent Jesus to be my personal Savior. I understand as a Christian, I was not promised that I would never have problems, but I was promised that He would never leave or forsake me. This assurance was the only way I could have made it through my cancer battle.

My medical treatment started with 18 weeks of aggressive chemotherapy. This protocol helped immensely but did not do the job completely. I still had a resistant pocket of cancer that had not responded. The next step was an autologous bone marrow transplant in which my own bone marrow would be harvested and then transplanted via transfusion to replace the damaged marrow. The days after the transfusion were critical as the medical team closely monitored my blood count to see if it was starting to rise. Fortunately, my blood started building in the first few days and I was dismissed three weeks after the surgery, a record for that time.

After the ordeal, I was very weak but I gradually started rebuilding my strength. I began by walking daily; then mixed in a little running; and then went back to daily running. It took determination and lots of support from my wife and family. I returned weekly, then monthly, then quarterly, then biannually and finally annually for checkups. After five years, my doctors pronounced me "cured" and released me. "Praise God from whom all blessings flow!"

It has been over fourteen years since my transplant. I have a website, www.inspirezone.org, which covers a number of subjects, including cancer. I am always happy to talk with other cancer patients to offer help and support any way I can.

"May you live to eat the hen that scratches on your grave."

—Carl Sandburg

*"Once you understand the worst,
you can fight the best fight."*

A Parent First

Craig Cooper

For me, the will to fight a deadly form of cancer came from two sources; a higher power and the power of family.

The hardest thing I've done in my life was tell my young sons that their father had metastasized melanoma—the most severe form of skin cancer—and that I might die within a year. That was what the doctors said in April, 1991. Our sons were 12 and 10 years old.

I had great medical care, but I believe there was much more to my story of survival. In my hospital bed during experimental treatments and following surgery, I wrote goals for whatever was left of my life in a journal.

Some of the goals were easy to accomplish, others were more complex and extravagant. I wrote that I wanted to see my sons graduate from high school and see them play more games. I dreamed that I would travel with my wife, fish again in Minnesota, and as totally improbable as it sounded at the time, I wanted to see my alma mater, Iowa State University, win a football bowl game.

I have been cancer free since 1992 after being told in 1991 that, statistically, the odds were that I would probably only survive nine months to a year. Most of the entries in the journal have been crossed out. My sons have both graduated from college. I've watched them compete in dozens of athletic events at the youth, high school and college levels. We have taken many family trips. I changed jobs and have spent much more time with Susan, my wife.

In 2004, both of our sons got married.

The point I would emphasize to anyone going through what I went through is that I had a strong belief in medical technology, but an even stronger faith in a higher power and the power of prayer. On the day I learned of my diagnosis, I got down on my knees and prayed. I felt an instant calmness that everything was going to be fine, regardless of my future. I believe that once you understand the worst, you can fight the best fight. That day on my knees, with tears running down my cheeks, the fear of cancer and fear of death disappeared. The promise of eternal life allows you to approach life fearlessly, which I've tried to do.

There are wonderful mysteries in survival. By surviving, I have been able to talk with other cancer patients who wanted information and reassurance. I have written a book and contributed to others. I don't understand why I survived and probably never will, but maybe it was to help others deal with their own fears.

My advice to anyone who calls is usually the same: find the best treatment and medical advice; go into the process with an open, determined mind; and never ever underestimate the awesome combined power of prayer and the human spirit.

"The whole ordeal brought out strength in us we didn't know we had. We now walk closer to one another and closer to God."

New Compassion for Life

Debi Linker

Until one has experienced a relentless course of medical procedures, you can't really understand the heel-kicking joy that comes with finishing the final treatment. The elation of completion is beyond words.

On October 13, 1998, I had my last regular lab and had completed a regimen of chemotherapy, radiation and surgery for breast cancer with lymph node involvement. HALLELUJAH! I was done. I had made it. Time to celebrate.

I learned a lot during my illness. I learned that God was in control and watching over us. My husband, Jim, and I literally felt the prayers of others upholding us and keeping us from despair. Our faith and our marriage were challenged, deepened and cemented in ways we could not have imagined.

For example, because of a commitment to teach, I had to have no delays in my last chemo. This required white blood cell stimulator injections. Jim, who always went faint at the site of a needle, now decided he would administer those injections to me. He came through with flying colors even though I often had to remind him "to breathe" during the course of the very slow injections. My hero! That's just one example of how the whole ordeal brought out strength in us we didn't know we had. We now walk closer to one another and closer to God.

Another thing that helped was a book my doctor recommended in advance of surgery: Dr. Susan Love's "The Complete Breast Book." It's full of all the information anyone would ever need about breasts, cancer and treatments. As far as I'm concerned, it's a must read for any woman, whether or not she is in the throes of breast cancer.

For me, makeup also proved to be a very important asset during chemotherapy. Anyone in this phase who's interested should call the American Cancer Society and ask for the Look Good, Feel Better volunteer. They provide makeup sessions for cancer patients and even leave you with lots of top name cosmetics. It certainly helped me look and feel better.

The other thing I discovered as a result of my breast cancer and my treatments is the value of good health and physical strength. I now am a serious walker. I use my walking to help raise money for breast cancer. I have walked in four Avon events raising over $20,000 for breast cancer in the past four years. I am hoping to walk with my friend Polly Letofsky across Michigan and Wisconsin this year. She is the driving force behind Globalwalk, which raises both funds and awareness for breast cancer.

In facing my mortality, I have learned a new compassion for those who suffer with life threatening diseases and have gained a new appreciation of those who are trying to raise funds to help find the cures. I have become a giver of myself and my talents to benefit others. I know that this experience has left me a better person.

The illness is dangerous, but I am more dangerous than the illness."

—Paramahansa Yogananda

"I never thought about dying. It was not an option."

Unstoppable Life

Tiffany Buckmiller-Sutton

I had been really sick for about two months, and the doctor at the college I was attending first diagnosed me as having depression. My symptoms included extreme weight loss, loss of appetite, night sweats and crying spells. It turned out that, at 21, I was suffering from Hodgkin's Lymphoma—stage IVB.

My family was hysterical when they found out. After the doctor left my hospital room everyone went berserk. I cried a bit and then just had this calming sensation come over me and the thought that I was going to be OK. I then asked the doctors if there was anything they could do for me there before I went to the Cancer Center the next week. They said no. So I told them I wanted to go home right then, and I did.

At the Cancer Center they told me that the cancer was all through my body and into my bones. I was producing no blood, which was why I was so anemic. Even though Hodgkin's is said to be one of the most treatable cancers, at this stage we could only hope and pray.

I was told that I would need 6 months of chemo and that I might not be able to have children afterwards because chemo puts a lot of women into early menopause. A lot to accept at 21.

But I said, "Let's do it."

And I did go through it! It was not easy but I had a lot of support from family and friends and I never thought about dying. It was NOT an option. I got lots of rest, ate homemade meals; my father would make me walk around the house no matter how much it hurt. Believe it or not, once I started chemo I began to get stronger. I've been way sicker with a hangover than I ever was on chemo.

Once I was strong enough (about 2 months into chemo) I began to live life like I did prior to cancer. I would go to bars with friends; rollerblade; water ski and hike. I don't recommend this, but I did everything the doctors said not to do and ate everything they said not to eat. I visited my grandparents every day and would play cards with my grandmother for hours. My boyfriend of 4 years couldn't handle my cancer. It was over for us and that was very hard to deal with while going through chemo. But life goes on, and that's just what I did.

Three months into chemo, to the amazement of everyone, the cancer was gone. It was a miracle! I still went through the remaining three months and as soon as it was done, I jumped right back into life. I moved away from home and got an apartment with a friend. I got a job waitressing while I was still bald. I got some pretty strange looks and comments, but I didn't care. In the process I met my husband, who was everything I wanted. We were engaged and living together when we found out we were pregnant.

It's been eight years since my initial diagnosis, and we just found out that I'm expecting again. There are no guarantees in life, only what we make of it. And I plan to make the most of it!

"Never give up. Take one surgery, one treatment, one test at a time."

I Can Survive

Diane S. Thompson

August: "How are we going to tell her?" Trying to wake up from hours of anesthesia, every inch of my body aches and I feel tubes in my side and oxygen on my face. In the distance I hear the voices of my sister and my husband. I have cancer and they are afraid to break the news. I drift back to sleep and the next face I remember is the doctor's. He goes into detail about the surgery and my diagnosis. There are cancer cells in my abdominal cavity and on my liver. I will need chemotherapy and lots of care for the next year.

This was the beginning of my journey to being a Stage III, ovarian cancer survivor. Three weeks after the surgery, chemotherapy began with large doses of Taxol and Carboplatin. I spent a lot of time reading about cancer. Ovarian cancer survivors seemed to be few and far between.

October: I joined the "I Can Cope" class at the hospital. How wonderful to find 15 people who were all surviving cancer. Over the next couple of months we became close friends who laughed, cried and learned together. These became "my people."

December: I'm very weak and feel very ugly. I would stare in the mirror many times that winter and wonder where Diane had gone. I was too sick to work and too weak to continue treatments. I did manage to bake my usual Christmas cookies and have the family in for our traditional Christmas Eve meal. After the holidays, my blood rebounded and treatments resumed.

February: CT scan revealed a remaining tumor and the need for more chemotherapy. I wanted to return to work, so for the next eight weeks I worked four days and went for chemo on Fridays.

June: Tumor is still there. I need a "second look" surgery; I am so tired of looking at cancer. Once again the doctor will cut me open, remove tumors, biopsy organs and do chemical washes of my insides. I pray a lot and am trying not to give up. This time they attach a gismo to my ribs to deliver chemo to my abdominal cavity every three weeks for the next seven months. I take another leave from work. Friends and family think the end is near, but I am determined that if anyone can survive, Diane can.

I continue to surround myself with cancer survivors by staying in touch with my "I Can Cope" friends and getting involved in the *Relay for Life*. I see hundreds of survivors and dream of soon being one.

December: I hear that wonderful word, "Remission."

I have been in remission now for three years. The 18 months I fought for my life are still a very clear memory. I have a one-word message to all cancer survivors: HOPE. Never give up HOPE. Take one surgery, one treatment and one test at a time.

"I think it was easier to deal with the pain and emotion of cancer as a kid. Children are a lot tougher than most people realize."

When I Was Ten

Christopher M. Brown

It was Easter morning, 1980. I was 10 and instead of taking a bite out of a chocolate bunny or eating too many jelly beans, I was awaking from surgery dazed and confused. The surgeons had just removed a malignant tumor which had been discovered while the doctors where trying to determine the cause of my acute stomach pains.

The news was bad. They determined I had 6 weeks to live. They suggested I be taken to see the oncologists at Emory University in Atlanta. I don't know if you can imagine what it felt like being a 10-year-old whisked south in an ambulance on 1-85 from Greenville, South Carolina just a few days after surgery. Weird!

There was better news from the Emory doctors—the cancer hadn't spread and they started me on a strict regimen of chemotherapy. Even at that age, I realized I was lucky—luckier than a lot of other kids there. The problems and treatments went on for two-and-a-half years and included radiation, bone marrow transplants, spinal taps, blood transfusions, pneumonia, x-rays, CAT scans, collapsed veins, loss of hair and vomiting. The only constant was

PAIN. Towards the end I really felt like I was at the end of my rope. Fortunately it was also the end of my bout with cancer.

I am now 35 years old, happily married and cancer free since my childhood. I think it was easier to deal with the pain and emotion of cancer as a kid. Children are a lot tougher than most people realize. I don't remember a lot of what happened during my cancer battle. I have blocked a lot from my memory and as a result haven't reflected very much about that time in my life as an adult. Over the years, my family has filled in some of the details.

Every once and a while, though, I will experience a particular smell or sound and the memories come crashing back like a speeding train. I eventually shake it off, thank God to be alive and go on with my day. There is so much to be thankful for. I am thankful to God for giving me the will (and the miracles of medicine) to recover. I am grateful to my mother for being the strongest person I know. When told her child would die, she just wouldn't accept it as a possibility and willed our family through those difficult years.

I only hope that others can relate to my experiences and know they are not alone. As someone who spent almost 3 years of his childhood dealing with cancer, I offer this message of hope to kids and their parents currently dealing with the disease. Kids are tough. Kids do move on from cancer to have normal, healthy lives and to be thankful for every day of them. I'm one of them and I know.

"Everyone's path will be a little different, but the answer most likely lies in tapping into reinforcing energy from every possible source."

Positive Transformation

Rachel Clearwater

I had my breast removed in 1994, three days before my forty-ninth birthday. In the days immediately following my surgery, the entire experience seemed surreal, as if it were happening to someone else and I was an outside spectator looking in. I have since referred to this time as my "dream walk."

When this protective phase subsided, however, the stark reality of breast cancer set in, and I was gripped by the most horrendous terror I had ever encountered. I was so haunted by fear of a recurrence that sometimes I literally could not function. But, as a survivor, what I want every woman to know is that these feelings aren't permanent. They will pass.

With the passage of time, my heart again began to dance and a place deep inside my spirit was awakened—a place I feared had forever been lost. The good days began to outnumber the bad. One morning I was standing in the kitchen brewing a pot of green tea when I realized that I had gotten out of bed without the sudden shock wake of remembrance.

From that moment on, my life started to undergo a positive transformation.

I did everything I could possibly do to empower myself and stack the odds more favorably in my direction. I found the Center for Attitudinal Healing, a non-traditional support group. I also put myself into therapy to deal with the various stressors in my life, realizing that sometimes those outside our immediate circle can help to put experiences in a different and more enlightening perspective.

I also changed my diet, listened to guided meditations such as "Invitation to Healing" and "Morning and Evening Meditation" and made a point to seek out books written with a healing focus and filled with help and hope. Among my all-time favorites: "The Breast Cancer Prevention Diet" and "Love, Medicine and Miracles."

Everyone's path will be a little different, but the answer most likely lies in tapping into reinforcing energy from every possible source.

Since that November day, almost eleven years ago when I had my mastectomy, I have celebrated my 30th wedding anniversary, watched my grandchildren grow, made wonderful new friendships and listened to Chopin and Massenet with my dog nestled gently in the crook of my arm. I even wrote a book about my breast cancer experience, "Dreamwalk, A Survivor's Journey Through Breast Cancer."

Every day is now precious—a gift to be unwrapped and savored from the depth of my spirit. I will continue living in this place of gratitude, this place which God has allowed me to have for this moment and hopefully for many more to come.

"Our powerful and loving God answers prayer and delivers us from hopeless situations."

Why Chaplain Tim Wears a Ponytail

Timothy Herron

A lot of people ask why a seemingly conservative hospital chaplain like me wears a ponytail. There are two answers—one practical, the other a testimony to the greatness of God.

During the 1988 Christmas season I began to have bad headaches which grew excruciating. The cause proved to be a fourth degree malignancy or glioblastoma multiforme, the deadliest form of brain cancer. The first year survival rate is less than 1%.

My congregation, Fellowship Bible Church, refused to accept this prognosis and devoted themselves to praying for me and my family. They got the word out far and wide and calls and notes flooded in from individuals, families, churches and schools who were in prayer for us. Thousands of tiny pins covered a map in the foyer of our church representing this amazing worldwide prayer network.

On the medical front, doctor friends put me in touch with one of the country's leading neurooncologists who, despite his knowledge and access to the latest medical advances, gave me little chance of surviving even the first six weeks of radiation therapy. This was a really low point for us all. So God's people continued to pray...and God provided a neurosurgeon who believed a second craniotomy might be able to remove the lion's share of the tumor. The surgery was as successful as it could be; but it was highly likely that a few renegade cells escaped the procedure and they were all that would be needed for the cancer to return with a vengeance. So massive radiation aimed at that tumor was the next step. It resulted in a bizarre and unsightly pattern of balding. After some experimenting, I discovered that if I grew my remaining hair long, gathered it back and tied it in a ponytail, I could successfully conceal the patches.

So now you know why I wear a ponytail. But that's not the whole story....

Radiation implants were the one treatment that held out the most promise for a long-term cure. The implants would hopefully attack any and all cells in their path; and so over 6800 rads were delivered to the depths of my brain. Despite great concerns about serious brain damage, I only experienced slight neurological deficits which, considering everything, are insignificant.

Almost 15 years have passed since the initial diagnosis and gloomy prognosis. During the whole time I have been sustained by the Lord and those who love me and have rarely been out of the pulpit. The impact on the lives of others in hearing my story has made the whole ordeal worthwhile to me, my family and my church. And my ponytail? It remains a testimony to our powerful and loving God who answers prayer and delivers us from hopeless situations. I urge all looking for hope to contact me at Overcomers, Inc.

Editors Note: With age and time, Chaplin Tim has chosen to lose the ponytail and happily sport a bald head as a living reminder and witness of God's grace to him.

"Don't ever give up. Look into all alternatives."

A Clear Alternative

Helene Hendrixson

The news I got in January, 1997 couldn't have been worse—stage IV non-Hodgkins Lymphoma or NHL. NHL has become one of the fastest growing types of cancer, with approximately 50,000 new cases each year. When caught early, NHL will usually respond well to traditional therapies like chemo and radiation.

That wasn't the case for me.

My cancer was really advanced and the doctor advised me that chemo is never a cure for NHL and eventually will not work. In fact, once you introduce it into your body, the next time it will not be as effective. My doctor suggested I enter a clinical trial. However, it only had a 5% chance of giving me any real benefits. But I'm not the kind of person to give up easily. I don't throw in the towel without putting up a good fight and that probably saved my life.

A few weeks later, my aunt and uncle called to tell me they had heard of an alternative treatment that used the mineral cesium and also the whole leaf of the aloe vera plant. They said that there seemed to be some pretty good success traced to this approach. So I started the cesium according to the High pH protocol. The following month I began taking the aloe vera concentrate.

As I learned more and more about the clinical trial, I became less and less enthusiastic about participating. I was also seeing clear evidence that the alternative therapy was working. Just a month after starting the cesium, the lumps in my lymph nodes were down. During the next year, two times I tried going off the supplements but after a few days the lymph nodes would swell so I would go back on the supplements and the swelling would go down. After a year of starting the procedure, the swollen lymph nodes had completely disappeared. But this was my life and I had to be sure it was the cesium and the aloe vera that were doing the job.

When the tumors were gone for a couple of months, I decided to stop the cesium and stay with only the aloe vera concentrate. This time the tumors didn't return. Today, more than seven years after being diagnosed with "death sentence" NHL, I am still cancer free. I took no chemo, no radiation, no therapies other than the cesium and aloe.

I also changed other things in my life. I put myself on a healthy diet, got rid of all products both food and cosmetics that weren't natural, practiced meditation and visualization to focus on my body healing the cancer cells and, most important, had a large network of friends and family that constantly prayed for me.

Here's what I want to share with those in the throes of the worst types of cancers. Don't give up. Look into potentially life-saving alternative therapies. For me, I'm pretty sure that the alternative therapy approach, and my willingness to ask the right questions, even when I was at my sickest, saved my life.

"Watching the birds and squirrels at play was therapy for my soul and mind, as well as my body."

Shattered Glass (Almost)

Michelle Murphy

Diagnosis on admission: uterine fibroid(s). Discharge diagnosis: ovarian cancer. The silent killer. My oncologist described the nature of this cancer as "angry, aggressive and insidious." The plan: to attack an aggressive cancer with aggressive chemotherapy as soon as I recovered sufficiently from surgery.

My family had moved a day bed to our sun porch so, as I healed from surgery, I could absorb the heat of our warm Carolina sun. Watching the birds and squirrels at play was therapy for my soul and mind, as well as my body.

When I lost all my body hair during chemo, it was more a curiosity than a concern. I made scarves out of well-chosen pieces of fabrics; penciled in eyebrows and thought I looked pretty good. I was determined not to look sick, but sometimes in the hospital I would sink into nausea and drug induced oblivion. With time, I learned to transport my imagination through the skies, like Casper the Ghost and whisk myself away to the rugged coast of Oregon. I could also feel the prayerful energy of friends and family holding hands from coast to coast. I relied on these images well after ending the four-month course of chemotherapy.

The end of therapy brought some of my most significant challenges. My oncologist told me my survival chances were about 15% and my cancer would surely return. When I enrolled in a medical terminology course to better understand the language of medicine, the instructor re-affirmed the doctor's prognosis and described ovarian cancer as an "automatic death sentence." It also turned out my thyroid gland function was deteriorating and I found myself unable to hold a cup, a pencil or even stir a pot of soup. I went home and marked my belongings so my family would understand their history. Then I waited to die.

During a business trip with my husband, I had brunch with an acquaintance. She asked what my plans for the future were now that I had emerged from cancer. I told her I was going to die. She picked up her fork and crashed it down three times on the glass table making a terrible noise. I thought the table would shatter. She looked at me and said: "NO, you are NOT going to die." "I'm not?" "NO you are not!" We paid the bill and went shopping. That day was the turning point of my life.

I changed oncologists to one who was more encouraging and positive. He told me he believed I was here to do good. I know he's right. I got an Associate Degree in Human Services, attended numerous seminars on the psychosocial dimensions of cancer and got a job in bereavement counseling.

Today, more than 15 years later, I continue to be well and support cancer patients on a peer counseling basis. My life is full, as is my heart—thanks to the love and support of my son, his family, my husband and my friends.

"Remember, your mind is so much more powerful than your body!"

Angels Watching

Stacie Snyderburn

Three days before my 15th birthday in 1996, I was diagnosed with osteogenic sarcoma and I wasn't expected to make it.

Somehow though I was blessed.

They thought I would die of cancer and I didn't. They thought that the large tumor that had gotten to the bone and muscle of my leg would mean they'd have to amputate. Yet, I woke up from surgery with both my legs.

I was constantly sick and had every infection possible. So they thought the huge doses of chemo would kill me even before the cancer, but it didn't.

I would wind up spending three months at a time in the hospital for my chemo. As the oldest kid on the cancer floor (the others were between 1 and 12), I would visit them, play games and watch movies with them. We all had a bond and kept each other strong even though we were told we weren't going to make it. We made a promise that we would see each other in heaven. The 5 friends who looked up to me like a sister died within a month. I went to all 5 funerals and I was expected to be next. I am still here; still surviving; still living my life to the fullest.

While it's hard to stay strong during cancer, it's the best thing a person can do. Your mind is so much more powerful than your body. Keeping a journal helped me tremendously. Now, I look back and see that I beat it. Then, it was a big help in keeping my mind off things.

I had goals that I thought about often during my cancer and that kept me going. I wanted to someday have a family. I wanted to become a doctor or a nurse and help other cancer patients like my medical team helped me. Right now I am a third year nursing student at the University of Toledo.

Also it helps to know that there are five angels in heaven watching over me. Lexy, Andy, Anthony, James and JT. I will always remember the love we had for each other, and please continue to watch over me and keep me safe.

"My take-charge approach to personal healing brought me both hope and health."

My Way

Larry Clapp

My cancer-fighting approach was the same as my approach to business and life—take charge. As a lawyer, CEO and entrepreneur, this strategy had brought me both success and happiness.

So when in 1990 the doctors told me: "You are going to die a very painful death if we don't cut out your cancerous prostate, immediately," I refused to accept their recommendation of "minor surgery" as the only option.

I pressed for answers about side effects and learned I might become impotent, incontinent and that I would have to take eight weeks off to recuperate from this "minor surgery." These were unacceptable to me. So I decided to take charge of my disease myself and began an intensive exploration of alternatives. I talked my way into medical libraries and consulted with many MDs, biological dentists and healers of all types. I learned that prostate cancer occurs mainly in Western, developed countries and that nutrition is a major factor.

I went on a fasting retreat and saw the toxins come out of my body and saw my PSA come down from near 10 to near 5 in a single week. I knew I was on the right track because toxins were a major enemy of prostate health. Within two months, my PSA was less than 2 and I was cancer free.

My take-charge approach to personal healing brought me both hope and health. Thirteen years after my original diagnosis, I am cancer free. I have continued my research, cleansing and learning to this day and have intensively studied nutritional healing, pH balancing, herbology, homeopathy, bodywork and energetic and spiritual healing. Based on my research, I earned a Ph.D. in 1996 from London's Galien University.

I also am committed to helping others find paths that will work for them. I have written a book, "Prostate Health in 90 Days...Without Drugs or Surgery" and try to spread the word through my website, audiotapes and appearances on radio and television. I have also co-authored "Awaken the Healer Within" which focuses on the emotional aspects of healing. I coach men suffering from prostate problems, including cancer, and tailor versions of my plan to give each person the help he needs to deal with these life-threatening ailments.

In short, my take-charge attitude now drives me, as a prostate cancer survivor, to help others reverse prostate cancer without drugs or surgery.

"Positive anything is better than negative nothing."

—Anonymous

'ike Panther & family at son
yle's graduation

Paul & Jennie Leverett

Michelle Waters & daughter Macy

Ed Keelen with his family tailgating at a Clemson football game

Terri Bronocco Jones
w/dad in Italy

Tim Herron (in suit) and family

David Bradley & his girls

Jeanne Bonine with one of her paintings from the Jeanne Bonine Studio

Greg Fornelli

Rachael & Stan Clearwater

Lois Cook (second from left) with family (husband Jim)

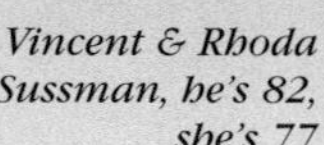

Vincent & Rhoda Sussman, he's 82, she's 77

Terry Healey with wife Sue

Michelle Murphy, sailing out of Southport, NC

ana Brabec and daughter, Kim

Polly Letofsky and Debbie Linker (on the right)

Joe Cunningham and granddaughter Ellexa

Vicki Tosher represents Colorado as an advocate at a 2002 National Breast Cancer Coalition rally in Washington, DC.

Linda Kedy with son, Jesse

Jamie Hutchings with her family

Larry Clapp – Crop skate

yn Phenix with her husband Paul

Anne McGown (left) and friend Dr Verushka Krigovsky in China, one year after having cancer.

Dr. Mike Retsky & Romano in Nice

Matthew Zachary performing

Harriett Coffey (in the pink shorts)

Annette Knowles & family

Tony Presley

Brent Barringer- he's in the light blue shirt

Robert Norcross – mountain biking

"Offset each negative experience with a positive one. Use fun as a way to get through the daily grind."

Together

Lois and Jim Cook

While it was Lois who was diagnosed with breast cancer, we view this experience as a journey we traveled together. We believe our loving relationship helped BOTH of us survive her cancer.

On his way home from work one Friday afternoon, Jim heard an NPR story about breast cancer and came home telling Lois about it. Having noticed a mass on her breast during a recent self-exam, Lois was prompted to schedule an appointment for a mammogram. Jim flew out for a brief business trip on Saturday and before he returned Lois had gotten a mammogram, a biopsy and a clear diagnosis. And our life changed. In the next two years, we would go through three surgeries, two rounds of chemotherapy and a series of radiation treatments.

Initially, we avoided talking about Lois' cancer to others. It was just too hard for them and for us. One of the best pieces of advice we received was from a friend who had lost his wife to cancer several years before. "If you don't let them know, they can't help you." His advice prompted us to maintain contact with family and friends, predominantly through email, which served three important purposes. It kept us connected; it allowed us to solicit help when we might not otherwise be comfortable asking; it allowed Jim to "talk" through HIS concerns and get a variety of perspectives.

Another decision we made early on was to make sure we didn't have our lives revolve solely around surgery, chemo and doctors appointments. To help us survive the everyday realities of cancer, we tried to offset each negative experience with a positive one. We had always talked about finding time to eat lunch together but our busy schedules seemed to always get in the way. So chemotherapy sessions became opportunities for "lunch dates" either before or after. Lois' daily trips to radiation treatments were accompanied by visits with friends who volunteered to transport her. Balancing the negative with something fun helped us get through the daily cancer grind.

We also continued to travel, a much-loved pastime, and didn't cancel already-planned trips. In particular, with the OK of Lois' doctor, we delayed her surgery for two weeks so we could go to Portland, Oregon on a business trip for Jim. Some people thought we were crazy to put off the surgery, but our surgeon assured us it would make no difference in the prognosis, so we took the time and made the trip. After surgery, Lois also continued with her plans to attend a much anticipated business trip of her own, which provided the added benefit of seeing old friends.

As a result of cancer, our strong relationship has become stronger. Our family is closer than ever and we learned better how to give and receive help. We urge all affected by cancer to accept the help of family, friends and support groups and organizations...and find ways to treat yourself well. You too will be a survivor.

"I found that after bladder cancer, even with an ostomy bag, I could live normally and I wanted to help other bladder cancer victims realize too."

A Player—Not Just a Patient

Vincent Sussman

I am 84 years old and a bladder cancer survivor.

Several weeks before my 80th birthday, a grade IV cancer was discovered in the muscle lining of my bladder. My son researched the Internet and discovered exposure to chemicals in the workplace as one of the likely causes.

As a research chemist and plastics engineer for fifty years, I had been exposed to chemicals, then thought to be harmless. Many were subsequently found to cause cancer. This was before OSHA regulations. My first message of hope is that's all changed. Today, chemicals used in the workplace must have MSDSs (Material Safety Data Sheets), which states the tolerance and risk factors associated with these chemicals and how they can be safely handled.

My bladder had to be removed and a piece of my intestine was used to conduct the urine through my abdominal skin into a plastic pouch. This is called an ostomy. The operation took 6 hours and I was in the hospital for 9 days. Fortunately, the cancer had not spread so I did not need chemotherapy.

While in the hospital I decided to document my experiences. I wanted to be a player, not just a patient. So I kept a day-to-day diary while I was in the hospital, as well as after I came home.

I stayed very upbeat during my recovery. I had a routine of walking the length of my house and increasing the distance as I became stronger. Just two months after my surgery, I wrote in my diary: "Today is beautiful. The sun is shining. It's 60 degrees. I go for a 2 mile walk and inhale the fresh air. I feel great; my life is returning to normal. I have survived cancer and expect to see the arrival of the millennium within a few weeks."

I found that after bladder cancer, even with an ostomy bag, I could live normally and I wanted to help other bladder cancer victims realize it as well. I decided to put my story on the Internet. With the help of my grandson, we designed a website. Within a few weeks, I started receiving messages. In 6 months I had received over 5,000 hits and about 300 emails from people wanting to chat with me. It was my pleasure to respond to them all, and give support and information. Many were from other countries including Australia, Canada, China, Greece, Iran, Italy, South Africa, Trinidad, Scotland and England.

Thousands of people each year are diagnosed with bladder cancer; most are over 50 with more men affected than women. The purpose of my website, www.angelfire.com/ct3/survivorofcancer is to give them and their families a chance to see that there is help and hope. Most of all, I look forward to more and more members in our site's bladder cancer "Survivor Club."

"If I had to live my life over again I would not change a thing, not even the leukemia, because of all the wonderful people that I met."

Caroline's Miracle—Part 1:

Before the Transplant

Caroline Strother

I'm 10 now. I was 2 years old and 4 months when I got diagnosed with ALL. ALL stands for acute lymphocytic leukemia. If you have to have leukemia it's the better of the bad types because it's treatable with chemotherapy. Or so we thought.

There are so many things I remember. But most of all I remember the people. I know this sounds really hard to believe but if I had to live my life over again I would not change a thing, not even the leukemia, because of all the wonderful people that I met. Like Ms. Arleta, the cleaning lady at the hospital.

I had just had surgery and was really sick. Every morning she'd come in and say, "Carolina, I am praying for you." I knew she really cared about me so it was OK she called me Carolina even though my name is Caroline. Dr. G, my doctor, he was really nice too. I called him Dr. G because his name was too hard for me to say. He always had toys around his neck and funny ties with cartoon characters.

I finally got to go home but my fever kept coming back. December 19th was a great day, because my leukemia was in remission and I was able to be home for Christmas. After Christmas, I had to go to the hospital for 4 days every 2 weeks for 6 months to get more chemo. The hospital was fun because there were videos and toys and other kids to play with.

Because of really nice people, we also got to do neat things for two summers. The first summer we got to go to a place called Jason's House in Myrtle Beach where my parents and I could stay for a week. Everything was free including the beach condo and amusement park rides. We all went, my parents, my 4 sisters and me. My favorite part was the amusement park. The next summer, we got to go to Disney World with Make A Wish. We stayed at Kid's Village where every family had a child with a serious illness. The best part was we never had to wait in line anywhere at Disney World.

The Leukemia came back though and I had to do hospital chemo for a second time. Nurse Chris was awesome. She gave me this super big syringe and told me to fill it with water and squirt Dr. G. I also squirted my dad. My Mom and Dad were very worried about me because this chemo was very strong and they had to decide on a treatment so the leukemia would not come back a 3rd time. If it did, I would have a very big problem.

Caroline's Miracle—Part 2:

The Transplant and Beyond

Caroline Strother

My Mom said I needed a bone marrow transplant at Duke Hospital so the leukemia would not ever come back. My parents said I would be at Duke for four months. We made seven trips there before my transplant in September. My friend Kelly, who I knew from the old hospital, was also having a bone marrow transplant at Duke. We saw her at Duke and she was in a lot of pain. A week later we found out Kelly had died. It was really sad and we went to her funeral. Duke could be a very sad place. Seven kids died during my four months there.

I had an umbilical cord blood transplant since none of my sisters or parents matched my bone marrow. The umbilical cord blood came from a girl in New York. One of the patient coordinators took digital photos of my transplant and we e-mailed it to all our friends. Eight days after my transplant the new white cells started to come in and everyone was happy. Two weeks after my transplant I got a 104°F fever. By the fourth week I felt really bad. Every time I went anywhere I had to drag my medicine tree. My Dad said I looked like a toxic waste site. Then I had seizures and a really bad reaction to the medicines. They moved me to PICU, a real scary place because the kids in here were almost at the point of death.

I guess it was worth it because after that my white blood cells started to grow back fast. After 48 days in the hospital I got to leave. One of the nurses told me leaving the bone marrow unit alive was a really big deal. The University Inn was like my new home and I got to know everyone who worked there. They were great. The girl next door to me, Brooke, also had a transplant. I had to go to the clinic everyday except Saturday and Sunday to be checked by the transplant doctors.

Well, Christmas was almost here and the doctors said I could go home early since I was doing so well. There were many people as we drove up the main road with signs that said "Welcome Home Caroline." It was really neat.

It took over a year for me to be off all the medicine and for my body to heal. My parents and I have been in two movies on umbilical cord transplants that were shown at the American Cancer Society's *Relay for Life*. I got to walk in it and it was so much fun, but I had to wear my mask every time I left the house.

Today I lead a normal life playing soccer and going to school. To everybody who helped me do that:

Thank You!!!!!!!!!!!!!!!!!!!!!

"Some people are like tea bags. They never know how strong they are until they get into hot water."

—Unknown

"Positive, constructive thinking fights cancer—no doubt about it."

Rebirth

Harriet Coffey

I had lived a charmed life. I was someone who had gone through a lot and always came up smelling like a rose, not the least of which was being a highly recognized radio personality. So when the doctor told me I had cancer, it was like he was talking to someone else. The initial shock knocked me down for a second and I openly wept. After I finished crying I thought, "That certainly didn't get me anywhere." I'm very much a fighter and I said to myself:

"Think about this instead."

The doctor whom I had selected to do my supposed "hernia" surgery was caught up in an emergency and so a different doctor performed it. As a result, the doctor I got by default was the only one in the surgical practice who knew about the rare cancer of the appendix that turned out to be my diagnosis. I thought about that a lot and decided God wanted me to stick around for a while. I believed something more was destined for me than I realized and I would beat the cancer. It's not that I'm very religious, either. Spiritual, yes, but I'm not a part of any organized religion.

I also thought about my son, Ryan, who at 26 had his whole life ahead of him and I wanted to see it unfold. I didn't have any grandchildren yet. He was a wonderful musician about to come into his own as a recording artist. There was so much to live for. It just couldn't be up yet. I didn't feel it was time for me to make my exit. I believed then—and I believe now—that there are bigger things planned for me and that's why I survived.

I also surrounded myself with amazingly positive people who were very encouraging—my family, my dear friends. At the time I was undergoing chemo, a good friend would lovingly lambaste me with the phrase, "Patience, Prisceldi." It was a nonsense name that served as her reminder to me that it would turn out OK; but I couldn't always have what I wanted when I wanted it.

A bright and shining moment for me was my son's taking six weeks off from his job as a social worker for the state of Connecticut to come take care of me. I thought, "Wow, isn't this a 360? HE'S taking care of me." I raised him on my own and it spoke volumes about who he was.

Now I'm the post-Cancer Harriet and I don't "sweat the small stuff" anymore. Cancer feeds off of negativity and stress is a form of negativity. Positive, constructive thinking fights cancer—no doubt about it. It helps in climbing any mountain. As a motivational speaker that's the message I want my audience to hear. It's the message I want anyone in the throes of cancer to hear.

"I urge all in the throes of cancer to see it, not as a death sentence, but as a sentence to live life like you've never lived it before, making important action and attitude changes every step of the way."

Dancing With The Diagnosis

Michelle Waters

On February 26, 1997, my guardian angels were working overtime. For no other reason than having a little extra time on my hands, I decided to go for my annual physical with the hope of being able to laud my lower-than-his cholesterol level over my husband. Two weeks and two specialists later, I was diagnosed with acute promyelocytic leukemia (APL). My dance with cancer had begun.

I sobbed. My husband shouted. My mother cried. As word of my diagnosis spread, I was showered with an avalanche of books and suggested readings with words like "cancer" and "healing" in the titles. "But when did I get into that category? Since when did cancer books apply to me?" As I began to skim the books, I became even more overwhelmed. Too many words. Information overload. I needed snippets, not details. I needed inspiration and hope, not mountains of scientific and therapeutic terms. I thought if I needed less, others did too. So I started to write down my own process of healing, learning and adapting, my own approach to *Dancing with the Diagnosis*.

For me, regaining some sense of control after "The News" was crucial to my sanity, my survival and my successful fight against the disease. Because it was difficult for me to fully comprehend my diagnosis on a scientific level, I was satisfied leaving the Physical Me to the physicians. To achieve balance, however, I dubbed myself Chief Executive Officer of the Emotional and Spiritual Me. I investigated complementary forms of healing — from meditation to homeopathy. I steadfastly practiced positive thinking and prayer, and I sought stable shoulders big enough for me to lean on when necessary. My new "promotion," spurred by a change in perspective, granted me a portion of the control and participation that I desperately sought.

Many people believe cancer is a death sentence. I chose, and urge all in its throes, to see it as a sentence to live life like you've never lived it before, making important action and attitude changes every step of the way, no matter what the prognosis. A cancer diagnosis powerfully signals us that it is time to heal, time to learn and time to teach.

It's been several years since my diagnosis. I'm in remission and plan to stay that way. In June of 2001, my husband and I welcomed our glorious daughter, Macy, into our lives. She is the epitome of health, hope and healing. Our son is due this fall.

Today I offer my book, *Dancing with the Diagnosis: Steps for Taking the Lead When Facing Cancer* (Rising Star Press), as an antidote for information overload. Activities, examples and affirmations demonstrate how a change in communication and perspective can empower those who feel powerless as they face cancer. My message to anyone dealing with disease is to dance that dance and always remember to LEAD!

"If you ask me what gave me strength to deal with these trials, I can honestly say it was the 3Fs: faith, family and friendships."

Conquering Fear, Conquering Pain

Annette Knowles

I was 31 years old and just beginning my master's program at the University of South Florida when I noticed how easily I became tired and out of breath and that I had some small bruises on my chest. At the insistence of my family, I went to the emergency room.

It turned out to be acute myelogenous leukemia (AML). My platelet count was 30,000 and should have been at least 140,000. I then had to make a decision: did I want conventional therapy or to be part of an aggressive chemotherapy clinical trial? I went for the clinical trial. I was in the hospital for about five weeks and experienced every possible side effect: nausea, diarrhea, vomiting, chills, fevers of 105 and hair loss. I remember feeling so unattractive, but always trying to stay optimistic and keep a smile on my face. Don't get me wrong, though. I did experience depression and roller coaster emotions as well.

Before this whole experience, my worst fear was pain. Not only did I face it; I conquered it. I'm no longer afraid of it or of dying. I believe no one is guaranteed tomorrow and we need to treasure every second of every day we have with each other.

After my third round of chemo, I chose NOT to have a bone marrow transplant mainly because I so desperately wanted to have children and all the chemo could render me sterile. Two years and 18 bone marrow biopsies after my third round of chemo, I was given a clean bill of health and told I could start trying to get pregnant; and I did, the very first time we tried. I now have an amazing son, Alexander. But my survivorship story doesn't end here. Eight months after our son was born, my husband was diagnosed with a rare heart disease and at the age of 28 had to have a defibrillator implanted. While it's not immediate, there is the possibility that he will eventually need a heart transplant.

If you ask me what gave me strength to deal with these trials, I can honestly say it was the 3Fs: faith, family and friendships. My faith in God helped me walk through the valley of the shadow of death. My family, especially my husband and mom, helped me stay strong through my most difficult hours. My friends held a blood drive to keep my blood transfusion and platelet bags full and sent hundreds of well wishes and prayers.

We really count our blessings now. We look at our beautiful son and thank God for sending him into our lives. Alexander is my heart outside of my body. My philosophy now fits the phrase: "Live, laugh and love." My theme song is Gloria Gaynor's "I Will Survive." If one person hears my story and says, "I can do that too," it is so worth it.

"There is no living thing that is not afraid when it faces danger. True courage is in facing danger when you are afraid."

—The Wizard, The Wizard of Oz

"I was in healthy denial. I was firmly convinced I was not going to die; not going to let this disease kill me."

Healthy Denial

Roger Haynes

I'm not sure what my wife's thoughts were; I'm not even certain what mine were. I do know I was in denial, but I think it was a healthy denial. I was firmly convinced I was not going to die; not going to let this disease kill me.

I was diagnosed with a Stage IV, small cell, Pancoast tumor in the upper lobe of the left lung which had spread to the left shoulder and was encasing the subclavian artery, the main blood supply source to the left arm. I underwent six weeks of pre-operative chemotherapy and 25 radiation treatments. Unfortunately, the treatments failed. Not only had the cancer not shrunk, it had spread to the brachial plexus area. My medical team concurred that the tumor was inoperable and probably incurable and estimated my life expectancy to be somewhere between six and nine months. They suggested I resign my job, get my financial and personal affairs in order and enjoy what time I had left.

I had to find a way to defeat it. My first step was to quit smoking and end a 35-year addiction to nicotine. My next step was to find doctors who would offer me some hope of survival. My chemotherapy and radiation oncologists agreed on an approach that included both types of treatment, scheduled over eight months. The treatments decreased the tumor by 40%. When the shrinkage stopped, we discontinued treatment and gave my body a chance to heal.

Every month I was feeling better and better. My regular visits with the oncologist were getting scheduled further and further apart. However, from October 1998 to September 2002, I continually refused to allow any type of scan or MRI. Finally, due to some numbness in my left shoulder, I decided to see what I looked like inside. X-ray, MRI, C-Scan and PET-Scan found no evidence of malignant growth.

The word "Remission" has never been used by me or my doctor. It's now been five years since my diagnosis and I live a happy and normal life, with no evidence of cancer. I owe my recovery and my life to my doctors, my wife, my prayers and those of family and friends. I also owe it to my attitude of healthy denial which made it impossible for me to accept my cancer as a death sentence.

"Battle scars make you realize how precious life is. Battle scars prepare you for whatever lies ahead."

Beyond Face Value

Terry Healey

At 20, my life had been smooth sailing. A junior at the University of California at Berkeley, I was confident, athletic, doing well at school and considered handsome. I had even been the homecoming prince back in high school.

Young, confident and "immortal," I didn't think much of a bump on my nose but had it removed and biopsied anyway. It turned out to be a tumor, a rare fibrosarcoma. With only a few post-surgery sutures, I returned to classes looking like I had been in a fight with someone, not something. Six months later I discovered that my previously unthreatening tumor had procreated itself into a horrific, life-threatening and potentially disfiguring malignancy.

I was too young to contemplate dying, but the realization that I could be disfigured was devastating. When I woke up from surgery, half my nose and upper lip were gone, the muscle and bone from my right cheek had been excised and the shelf of my eye, six teeth and part of my hard palate had been removed. My doctor's only promise was that he would make me "streetable," his way of preparing me for a lifetime of disfigurement.

When I was released from the hospital and the protection of my hospital room, I noticed adults staring and children laughing at me. A few of my friends and acquaintances were inadvertently negative. All of which left an indelible mark on my self-esteem. As a result, I would constantly seek reassurance from people. Did my looks bother them? Did they like me? How COULD they like me?

Five years and 20 attempts to reconstruct my face later, I was still coping with insecurity. In the hospital for my last reconstructive treatment, I met a fellow patient and we began dating. One day, after listening to me ask her how she felt about my looks for the umpteenth time, she ripped into me. The bulk of my problem, she said, was not my appearance, but my insecurity. Her honesty made me realize that surgery wouldn't fix the mental and emotional scars that had become far more disfiguring than my appearance.

That realization—along with prayer and the support of family and friends—worked to strengthen my spirit and my belief in myself. Out of my deep self-evaluation came the understanding that battle scars make you interesting. Battle scars make you wise. Battle scars make you realize how precious life is. Battle scars prepare you for whatever lies ahead.

Helping others became my greatest form of therapy. I volunteered at The Wellness Community, a cancer support organization for patients and their families and, by bringing them hope, began to feel better about myself.

Eighteen years after my cancer I am a successful marketing strategy consultant and professional speaker. I remain cancer free. I have written a book, "At Face Value," (10/2004) which shares my cancer story with others and hopefully provides a source of strength and hope as they deal with life's challenges and adversities.

"A reasonable amount o' fleas is good fer a dog—keeps him from broodin' over bein' a dog, mebbe."

—Edward Noyes Westcott (1847-98)

"I want to be remembered as someone who made a difference, who saved another man's life because he got tested after he heard about me."

The Grace of God and Doctors

Samuel P. Golden

I would not be here today if it were not for the care and diligence of my doctors and the grace of God.

At 45, after a routine physical, I was stunned to be diagnosed with prostate cancer. I knew little about the disease, but what little I did know, I presumed it happened only to men much older than I was. I know this sounds strange—and believe me, I love life—but I was never scared. I can honestly say that I didn't fear death. I thought more or less, what will be, will be. My concern was about my family, though. I didn't want to miss being here to watch them grow up and have families of their own. I had always planned on being here for them as they grew up. I didn't want them to have to go on without me.

My wife, Valerie, and I decided not to tell the children that I was going into surgery until almost the last minute. They reacted as well as could be expected…strong, bolstered by faith. This was the ultimate test of our family's faith. I simply told God that I trusted whatever He wanted would happen and that I was ready.

With that peace, I slept well the night before the surgery, so well in fact that Valerie had to move me along to get to St. Luke's in time for surgery. Surgery was the only course of treatment I ever seriously considered. I told the doctors to do the prostatectomy; to take it out because I didn't want the cancer growing back. When I woke up, Valerie was right beside me and I knew when I looked in her eyes everything was going to be OK.

And it still is OK, very OK, six years later. Cancer is a defining experience. Those of us who share this disease gain a new perspective on life. We see much more clearly what is important and what is not. I don't want to be remembered as a businessman or a negotiator; I want to be remembered as someone who made a difference, who saved another man's life because he got tested after he heard about me.

African American men have the highest rate of prostate cancer in the world. It accounts for almost 40% of the cancers diagnosed in us each year. We are more than twice as likely to have prostate cancer as white men; we are stricken earlier and we are more likely to die from it. I am dedicated to spreading the word about the importance of early detection for African American men. That's what we try to do with our website www.celebrateloveandlife.com.

Not a day goes by that I don't thank God for the opportunity to be here and I can tell you that I value every single moment I've been given.

"Cancer has taught me there are only two important things in life: love from the people around you and finding beauty in the smallest things."

The Warrior Princess

Jo Anne Daigre

Losing weight was the first sign that something was wrong. At first, I was proud of myself because I thought my diet was working, but then I started having trouble getting up for work or going jogging. I finally went to the doctor who gave me iron supplements, antibiotics and also did some blood work.

When I went back to the doctor he shocked me by asking if anyone in my family had leukemia and sent me to a hematologist. When he called with the results I was home alone. He told me that I had CML—chronic myelogenous leukemia; that there was no cure and that I had about three years to live. I asked him to refer me to the M.D. Anderson Cancer Center at the University Texas.

This was back in 1988 and Dr. Koller at M.D. Anderson gave me three choices. Do nothing and accept the 3-year-to-live prognosis. Take drugs that would improve my blood count but do nothing for the CML. Or, try a then-experimental drug, interferon.

Of course, I chose number three. The interferon was about what I call "managing misery." It made me ache all over like a bad case of the flu and some days I barely had the energy to get out of bed or to bathe. But it was the only choice then and I chose interferon's misery over death. I endured countless bone marrow aspirations. I did things to keep my mind and my spirits up. I had a poster of Zena, the Warrior Princess, which I used to remind myself of strength and of winning the battle - especially on the worst days. Today, I give these posters to women who have been diagnosed.

Things started turning around in the early '90's when I went into remission. I had a dream about beautiful flowers and a voice said in the dream, "they won't bloom unless you plant them." Despite my continuing exhaustion, I managed to begin a small garden around the base of a tree in my yard and found the more I worked the soil, the better I felt. There were years of ups and downs.

Then came 1998—a year of true tests. My mother died, my CML moved into an accelerated phase and I was headed for a blast crisis which signals the transformation from chronic to acute leukemia. My body was grieving for my mother. Then in January of 2000 right along with the new millennium came the light, the miracle. Dr. Koller at M.D. Anderson placed me in a new clinical trial for STI-571 (Glevac). After over 12 years of misery on interferon, I went into remission and started feeling like a normal person again.

No telling of my miracle would be complete without mentioning the blessings of dear friends who prayed for and encouraged me. They were always there whether I needed a small intimate conversation, or a party with the whole crew. They supported me with laughter, prayer, love, whole blood and platelets, and encouraging calls and cards. All of which I needed.

My 15 years with CML have been an involuntary spiritual journey. Now I KNOW that I know who I am. I know that love never dies. I know I am a lot like Zena. I am a warrior, an Amazon.

"I learned many things along my cancer journey: appreciate every minute of every day...take pleasure in every small achievement...never give up hope. Most of all, have fun."

Wellness: Beating the Odds

Norma Downes

My story might be quite different if I had access to the Internet in my rural Ontario, Canada home when I was first diagnosed with cancer back in 1991. I am amazed and heartened at the many resources now available. Back then, I was pretty much on my own in terms of finding support and protocols. A number of trips to Toronto and a variety of procedures revealed that I had Stage IV renal cancer, with the doctors referring to my condition as terminal.

From July to October, I had heard the words "terminal", "palliative" and "nothing else can be done" far too many times. It's amazing that I just did not go home and give up. Instead, I decided it was up to me to stay as well and as strong as I could. In essence, I chose to take control of the cancer rather than be controlled by it. I set up a daily schedule for myself that included rest, exercise, some change in diet, listening to relaxation tapes, time for the things I really liked to do and family time. I also tried to avoid stressful situations. In addition, I enjoyed "books on tape," especially "Head First: The Biology of Hope" by Norman Cousins.

Quite by accident, I found in an oncologist's office one day a brochure on a course called "Helping Yourself: A Cancer Coping Skills Training Program." It was being led by Dr. Allistair Cunningham, a former cancer patient himself, at the Ontario Cancer Institute. My husband and I signed up for a weekend course and we both found it very helpful. I was surprised to discover that much of what I built into my personal wellness plan was discussed at the course. We also met many supportive and caring people at the course. I learned many things along my cancer journey. I quickly discovered the importance of being my own advocate. I made sure my husband was with me at all appointments. That extra set of ears was invaluable during these stressful times. Like so many other people who have been diagnosed with so-called terminal cancer, I learned to appreciate every minute of every day. I now take pleasure in every small achievement and many of the things I used to think were so important in my life, I have now learned are meaningless. Despite the grim diagnosis and prognosis, I never gave up hope. I was quite open about my cancer which initially drove some people away. But now many of my friends thank me for my honesty as it has made it easier for them to talk to me and to others who have been diagnosed with cancer. Most of all, I have learned to have fun.

I am very happy to report there is still no evidence of the disease—this after that Stage IV diagnosis in 1991 when I was told I had six to twelve months to live. I am so glad to be alive and thank God for that every day.

"Never knock on Death's door. Ring the doorbell and run like hell, he hates that."

—Unknown

"Hope and the will to live are the foundation of the Healing Pyramid."

The Healing Pyramid

Bob Norcross

I was diagnosed with stage IV Renal Cell Carcinoma in June of 1999. At the time I was too stunned to be amazed, but the insidiousness of this disease is amazing to me now. It crept into my otherwise healthy body, leaving a 20 cm tumor in my right kidney; a 2.5 cm tumor on the right adrenal; 5 cm and 2 cm tumors in my left femur; and "numerous" lung tumors. Only weeks before I had been playing basketball in a senior's league, scrapping for rebounds with a left leg almost ready to snap. And I did NOT notice any decrease in lung capacity despite a chest full of tumors. In short, I was very active and unaware that I was about to get a death sentence. My first warning was nothing more than a type of pain I had not experienced before above my left knee.

Much has happened since then. I am still alive, contrary to the predictions of a prominent urologist. I am tumor-free at this time. My main reason for writing this piece is to provide hope for someone newly diagnosed, as I derived hope from reading Steve Dunn's web page (www.cancerguide.org) back in July of '99, when the specialists were getting me ready to die in 6 to 12 months.

A series of X-rays and tests pinpointed I had cancer and then the medical team had to go about determining exactly where the primary tumor was located. A CT scan confirmed that it was likely Renal Cell Carcinoma. One of the first procedures was to insert a metal rod to give my leg more strength prior to beginning radiation. It turned out to be especially painful since the surgeon inserted screws that were too long and resulted in abrading the flesh next to the bone. I opted to live with the pain for awhile.

About this time, a friend pointed me to several websites including Steve Dunn's. When I read Steve's and other stories I could relate to, it had an immediate effect on me as far as hope was concerned. If they could do it, I could do it too. At this point I also discovered that, although I was in the care of an outstanding medical facility, they were restricted as to which protocols they could use and basically they were suggesting nothing more than palliative care for my "death sentence" cancer. So I decided to visit the Center for Integrated Healing (CIH) in Vancouver, so I could combine alternative therapies with conventional ones. I also engaged in clinical trials for a drug called Pegylated Inferon alpha-2a, an 18-month protocol which, along with changes in lifestyle and diet, left me cancer free…but not problem free. Subsequently, I had eight leg operations with the ultimate outcome of an above-the-knee amputation.

But I am still very much alive and tumor free. Hope and the will to live are the foundation of the Healing Pyramid. Perhaps someone newly diagnosed with RCC will read this and derive the same hope I did when I read Steve Dunn's story.

"Don't waste time with self doubts and hindsight. There is nothing back there; your hope for survival is in front of you."

Defying the Odds

Kenneth Shapiro

There have been a number of theories, a lot of them off the wall, about why I am still alive more than 26 years after I received a cancer death sentence. The only thing that seems constant is that there is no scientific or medical explanation for my still being around.

When I was first diagnosed with metastatic melanoma Stage IV, the doctors told me I had two to three years to live and it kept going downhill from there. It went to two years, maximum. Then I was told, if I were lucky, I had thirty to sixty days.

However, I do have some thoughts about what may have contributed to my surviving. I learned early on that you have to be involved and totally aware of what is going on and why. Knowledge is the cancer patient's greatest ally. You have to know what questions to ask and not be afraid to ask them, over and over if you have to. What is being done and what results can be expected? In what period of time? How is progress going to be monitored? What happens if there are no results after we're half way through the program? The individual cancer patient has to be the main focus of the therapy. The medical side can't do it without the help of the individual; and the individual can't do it with the help of the medical side.

My definition of a good cancer patient—one with the best chance of survival—is someone who knows his or her disease and can discuss it with the physician as an equal, not an alien. Good cancer patients stand their ground and demand the information necessary that might just save their lives.

Once you have decided on your course of action, you must put 100% of your effort behind it. You must put 100% of your belief behind it. But also understand that getting down occasionally is natural and normal. We are not stones, and if we did not feel bad occasionally, we would not be human. You just have to be up and fighting the majority of the time. If you continually say things like; "Why I am doing this; it's going to fail anyway!" then it probably will. And, even when you've given it your best and it doesn't work, move on to something else. Don't waste time with self doubts or hindsight. There is nothing back there; everything is in front of you. That's where your hope for survival is.

Most of all, remember, it is NEVER over until you say it's over!

"I pray that after reading my story, stage IV patients will be able to look in the mirror and say: 'I CAN fight this and win.'"

Honeymoon Interrupted

Karen O'Neill Velasquez

In 1996 while I was on the beach in Santorini, Greece, honeymooning I was putting sunscreen on my face and felt a lump. Six years before I had a melanoma mole removed from my back.

I came home to discover that I was a stage IV cancer patient. I had a large tumor in my right jawbone and 32 lesions in the lymph system. There were also spots on my liver. As many of you know, stage IV is as bad as it gets and the doctors gave me a dismal diagnosis. I then had an experience no parent should have to endure. I had to tell my sweet son, Adam, about my illness. I will never forget that day.

I was not ready to give up. This just wasn't part of my plan. I had a nine-year-old son and a new husband. It was supposed to be a time to celebrate life…to enjoy all the good things life had to offer. I began to do research. My disease was very advanced and not operable, so I needed a systemic approach. My husband and I did our homework and came to the conclusion that the IL2/vaccine combo was what we wanted to do. The reason was simple. It had the best statistics for stage IV patients. I write about this approach to help buoy other stage IV patients who may be very fearful of IL2. Yes, it is difficult. Yes, the side effects can be brutal, but I came through it and did well…and you can too. After nine rounds, everything was gone from my body except the tumor in my jaw.

The doctors decided to remove my right jaw. It was a tough road back. I lost my teeth, the use of my tongue and all the feeling in my face. Then there was the whole reconstruction process. I was pretty ugly for a time there.

BUT……

Today, more than 7 years after my stage IV diagnosis, I am alive and doing well. I have two more children that we adopted and I feel healthy. Since the day of the operation on my jaw in 1998, I have been NEC (No Evidence of Cancer). I pray that after reading my story, stage IV patients will be able to look in the mirror and say: "I can do this. I can fight this and win." It's a bit easier to believe that when you actually know of someone who is doing well many years down the road.

Keep the faith! There can be lots of good life after a stage IV diagnosis.

"To me, every hour of the light and dark is a miracle. Every cubic inch of space is a miracle."

—Walt Whitman

"Cancer odds for survival are like tips from race horse buffs—most are wrong. The winners are usually the horses that people didn't believe rated a chance."

An Australian Story

Anne McGown

I grew up in Far North Queensland, Australia which has been touted as the "Skin Cancer Capital of the World" due largely to our beach-culture heritage. Since I viewed myself as olive skinned, I tended to ignore the mole just above my right clavicle which appeared to be getting bigger and more out of shape. I attributed the mole's changes to my gaining weight. It was getting fatter right along with me.

It really was my Dad's health problem that potentially saved my life. He was diagnosed with a stage II melanoma which required a wide incision to be removed. That was my wake up call. While he was recuperating at home in front of the TV, I snuck off to my local GP who did a biopsy. At 12:35 I received a call from him at work. Even before he said a word I knew it was bad news. Unfortunately, I was right…a melanoma for me as well.

It took four dialings for me to summon up enough courage to schedule my surgery. I kept hanging up. On the fourth dialing, I steeled myself up and made the appointment. I also spoke with my sister who was a nurse. "Should I cash in my chips, spend the lot and travel the world before I feel too sick to do it?" I asked.

"Only if you want to be a very hungry old lady," came her acerbic nurse's reply.

The surgeon did a very deep and wide incision right down to the bone. I know it sounds ghoulish, but for me it was important to take a look at what he cut out. The fatty white specimen was the size and depth of a large dessert spoon. I had expected to feel like I was looking into my own grave—but I didn't. The feeling was more akin to removing a large splinter—relief that it was out.

I call my scar my "tap on the shoulder." It is ugly and noticeable and I have no intention of having it revised by a plastic surgeon. When people stare I tell them what happened and offer to check their visible moles for them. Surprisingly, strangers don't back away; most have taken me up on my offer. I know I have had a potentially deadly cancer removed and had it not been for my Dad being the impetus for my getting the mole looked at, my life expectancy would have been cut way back.

My advice for anyone diagnosed with cancer is simple. Keep going in life. Cancer statistics, when applied to an individual's odds for survival, are like tips from race horse buffs—most are wrong. The winners are usually the horses that people didn't believe rated a chance.

"By overcoming my own despair and becoming my sick husband's advocate, I found two little-known treatments."

A Spouse's Story

Lydia Cunningham Rising

In September of 1984, my ex-husband, Joe Cunningham, was diagnosed with primary central nervous system lymphoma (PCNSL), a rare and deadly brain tumor with a survival rate of only 2-3% after five years. However, Joe has been in complete remission for almost 20 years now. He is well and fully functional working as a CPA/lawyer. In fact, since his recovery, Joe has been listed in the *100 Best Lawyers in America.*

Most importantly, he is still here to be with our children who are now in college. But it was a long journey from diagnosis to now.

When a CT scan at our local community hospital revealed a 3 centimeter mass in Joe's third ventricle, the neurosurgeons informed us it was inoperable and that at age 37, Joe should get his affairs in order. After a night of hysteria, I pulled myself together and decided to become Joe's advocate. If the worst did happen, I wanted to be able to look our two young sons in the eye and tell them that I had done everything I could to save their father.

My efforts would lead to two (then new) treatments which were unavailable in our home state of Michigan. One was at the Mayo Clinic. After a conversation with the doctor who was pioneering the procedure, Joe and I were on the plane to Minnesota within four hours. The long surgery was highly successful and resulted in 99% of the tumor being removed. The surgeon called it a miracle! Surgery was followed by radiation done close to home.

However, one month after the radiation, Joe started having headaches which were found to be caused by a second tumor. The Mayo doctors diagnosed it as PCNSL which tends to produce tumors in multiple sites throughout the nervous system. This time the neurooncologists at Mayo had little to offer. I returned to the medical library and after many hours of manual searching (no Internet back then!) I found an article written by a doctor at the Oregon Health Sciences University in Portland who was pioneering an approach to chemotherapy especially effective in treating PCNSL. So, now it was off to Portland!

It was well worth it. After only one treatment, 90% of the tumor was gone and after a second round, we never saw it again. Thus, by overcoming my own despair and becoming my husband's advocate, I had been able to find two very new and little-known treatments. Joe was one of the first 70 people in the U.S. to have the surgical procedure at Mayo and the tenth person to receive the revolutionary chemotherapy in Portland.

So, my overall message to you is—DON'T GIVE UP. Use all the resources available to you, which are far better than when I was helping Joe. If your physician is not aware of a treatment, make him or her aware of it. If they are still leery, check it out yourself. Investigators of clinical trials WILL talk to patients. For more information, I recommend the paperback book "Cancer Clinical Trials" by Robert Finn.

The best of luck to you!

"Cancer is a tough battle, but with the right attitude,
a battle that can be won.
Most importantly, it makes the real things
in life all the more precious."

The Real Things in Life

Ed Keelen

Two-and-a-half years after I was diagnosed with testicular cancer, my oncologist pronounced, "The tumor is gone." We had been through a lot together, but it wasn't over yet. Just a few months later, I was found to have a second cancer; this time of the prostate. Though different, each cancer played a role in making my value for the experience of living all the greater.

By the time my testicular cancer was discovered it had migrated to my stomach and was the size of a basketball. I ignored it because I thought I had inherited my father's middle-aged gut now that I myself was in my mid-50s. I felt no particular discomfort other than having to enlarge my pant size a notch and endure the gentle barbs of my wife. I finally went to my internist, who expressed concern and immediately ordered a CT scan, which showed the tumor in my abdomen. I was referred to an oncologist who determined that the cancer had originated in my right testicle. The day after confirmation of my diagnosis, I was on the operating table having my right testicle removed; and a week later I began the first of four rounds of chemotherapy.

While in the hospital recuperating from the surgery, I was in a great deal of discomfort. As I was trying to walk off the pain in the hospital corridor, a woman asked me how I was feeling. I replied, "Hanging in there," as a cover for the real pain. I watched as she turned and entered the room of her bedridden husband. His inability to get up really got to me. It put a whole new perspective on things. I COULD walk. I had my wife at my side and together we WOULD beat this thing.

I was on disability for seven months. I slept a lot, read a lot and grew spiritually. Each night before going to bed I would find great comfort from reading one of the Psalms.

The second cancer was discovered during a routine physical at work which showed elevated PSA levels. An ultrasound biopsy confirmed the presence of cancer in my prostate. It was considered completely separate and apart from the other cancer and this one was found early. I opted for nine weeks of radiation, which by comparison to the chemo was a cakewalk.

I have a sense of peace and calm about my cancers. I feel a renewed commitment to my wife of 31 years who never left my side. I still love work, but it is no longer all consuming. I cherish my visits with my children, the love of family and friends and the strength afforded by my faith. Cancer is a tough battle, but with the right attitude, a battle that can be won. Most importantly, it makes the real things in life all the more precious.

"In order to be a realist, you must believe in miracles."

—David Ben-Gurion

"Everyone says that I am strong, but I could not have done it without my parents, friends, family and teachers."

One Percent

Katelyn Scharlow

I was 12 when I found out that I had cancer. It all started with a pain in my left wrist, if I would bump it, it would hurt. I went to the emergency room to see what was wrong with it. They said that it was nothing and take some pain medicine. I took medicine but it still hurt so my parents took me to the family doctor. He said that it was gangly sis and sent me to Dr. Rao. Dr Rao checked it out and too said that it was gangly sis. He said that they mostly pop but if it got bigger, they would remove it. Well, it got bigger so I went back and got it taken out.

He said that it was a tumor but did not know if it was cancerous. However, he said he was 99% sure that it wasn't cancer. He sent it back to be tested and told me to come back in a week.

On October 23, 2000, we went back to Dr. Rao's office for the results. He came into the room with a sad look on his face and said those three devastating words. "You have cancer." It was Synovial Cell Sarcoma. Synovial Cell Sarcoma almost never happens to children. Out of that one percent of having it, I did. That night was also my dad's birthday. We had to go home and tell him that his daughter had cancer. What an awful birthday present that was.

On October 26, 2000, we had to go to Detroit Children's Hospital to get more tests done. I had to have a MRI, CAT Scan, Bone Scan and Chest X-ray. I then had to go for surgery to make sure they removed the tissue that the tumor surrounded. They tested the tissue and it came back negative for cancer. Dr. Mott said that I needed to come back from radiation in the "Cyclone" since there were only two machines like that, one being in Detroit and the other one in Washington.

So the first week of December, I went back to Detroit to get my radiation done. The Cyclone was a big circular machine with a door that was five feet thick. I was the only one left in the room with a camera and a microphone. I would sing to overcome my fears. This process went on for a week. There were a couple of good things that happened while I was up there, I did get to meet the Red Wings and see my family in Troy.

Dr. Mott said that I had to follow up with 5 weeks of radiation at home and said that I did not need chemo. So I did the 5 weeks of radiation and then we decided to get a second opinion on getting chemo. We went to visit Dr. Mitchell in Grand Rapids. She took my cancer research to the board and they agreed to give me preventive chemo for nine months. The chemo would make me sick; sometimes I could not eat and I also lost my hair.

At 14, I was done with chemo. My tests showed no sign of cancer. I finally got to be in remission. We had a big party to celebrate. Everyone says that I am strong, but I could not have done it without my parents, friends, family and teachers.

I'm 15 now and really active at school. I'm class president and a member of the student council and drama club. While I can't play sports because of the chemo affecting my lung capacity, I really support our school teams. This is also the third year I've led a team in the American Cancer Society's Relay for Life.

I feel so lucky to be blessed with great friends - they are the best.

"Anyone hearing the words 'You've got cancer' should know there is life after cancer and it can be very sweet."

The New Me

Mike Lachtanski

Life was going great for me. I had a good job, lots of friends, and I kept super busy with rock climbing, ice hockey, online gaming and fantasy sports. I worked hard and played hard, and never had enough time in the day. I was too busy to think about what life really meant to me and always buried my emotional issues deep down inside ...UNTIL ...I heard the wake-up-call words: "You've got cancer."

Always being a problem solver and now facing the biggest problem of them all, I felt I had to take charge of the entire process, even though I wasn't a doctor. I did my own research on Hodgkin's Disease. I found the treatment I wanted to go with at Stanford and made it happen, even without my local doctors help and approval.

The more I researched the specifics of fighting this disease, the more I realized I would also have to fight some of my natural instincts which would get in the way of my getting well. It is hard to address your own flaws, but I knew it was time for me to put the negative aspects of my life aside. I began to heal myself both spiritually and emotionally. I also came to the realization that I couldn't succeed alone.

I received enormous support from all my friends. Every prayer and kind thought made a difference and helped me overcome the challenges I faced as I underwent treatment during the most difficult period of my life from June to December of 1997. I experienced every side effect imaginable, but also came to realize that it was not a physical challenge at all, but a mental one. But I crossed the finish line and did so because I didn't try to make it alone.

That's why to this day, I try to help other patients. Having faced the challenges of Hodgkin's and its treatment, I can utter with absolute truth the words, "I understand." My website http://cybermage.netgate.net still has my daily journal of my experiences during treatment posted for all to read and hopefully be helped by it. I also answer every e-mail I receive from cancer patients or those caring for them. I'm not a doctor; I'm just one lucky guy, who happened to make enough friends in life to overcome a challenge he was not prepared for.

Yes. It's pretty amazing how things work out in life. If it weren't for my cancer, I wouldn't have married my wife, Karen, in May 1999. (She was trained to give shots that were part of my treatment.) Our wedding reflected our fun-loving approach to life and was quite different from your normal wedding ceremony. For example, we hired a troupe of actors to perform a murder mystery during our reception.

The "old me" who did everything on his own died to Cancer in 1997. The new me is very much alive and well. Those who hear the words "You've got cancer" should know there is life after cancer and it can be very sweet.

"Hope is about giving back; and I can think of no better way to give back than to fight for a cause which I believe can save thousands of lives."

Never Stop Searching

Mary Jo Siegel

In 1991, I was stricken with a fatal cancer, non-Hodgkin's lymphoma, for which no conventional cure yet exists. This disease is treatable for periods of time with chemotherapy and/or radiation, but the outcome is always death.

My husband Steve and I were devastated by my prognosis, but determined to find a cure. Our research took us to top lymphoma specialists at esteemed medical institutions around the country. All the experts confirmed our worst fears: with existing therapies, my disease was incurable. A ray of hope emerged with the recommendation that I undergo an autologous bone marrow transplant. This highly controversial procedure would require as much radiation as people who were within 1 mile of "ground zero" at Hiroshima. I was frightened and suspicious because only a handful of patients had survived this procedure with good long-term results.

Fortunately, we discovered the work of Dr. Stanislaw Burzynski who treated patients with advanced cancer using a gentle, non-toxic therapy he had discovered. As I began Dr. Burzynski's anti-neoplaston treatment, my lymphoma had progressed to a stage IV (there is no stage V). Malignant tumors were growing throughout my body. My bone marrow was infiltrated, and there was a large tumor growing on the side of my neck. After only 3 weeks on this medicine, that tumor disappeared! Subsequent scans showed continued reduction in tumor size.

During antineoplaston treatment, my quality of life was excellent, virtually free of side effects. I was an active and involved mother, an absolute necessity when you are raising three teenagers. More importantly, the drug stopped my supposedly terminal cancer. Within 12 months I was pronounced in remission, not by Dr. Burzynski, but by the same lymphoma expert who had originally diagnosed me and told me I faced certain death from this disease. I went off treatment and remained in remission for two years, when a follow-up scan revealed a possible return of the disease. Immediately, Dr. Burzynski prescribed a regimen of antineoplaston capsules. Within 5 months, I was once again in remission and have remained cancer free to this day.

Hope is about giving back and I can think of no better way to give back than to fight for a cause which I believe can save thousands of lives. As a result, I have become a vocal advocate for approval by the FDA of Dr. Burzynski's antineoplaston protocol. I have testified before Congress on this point and my testimony included the following statement:

> "Shouldn't it be the doctor, in concert with the patient, making important medical treatment decisions?... Because conventional FDA-approved remedies have failed to work for the majority of Dr. Burzynski's patients, often their only choice is antineoplastons or death!"

I am alive today because of antineoplastons and I look forward to the day when this vital weapon in the war against cancer is available to every single person who needs it.

I had my ups and downs, but I was never giving up hope and continue with a very good feeling about the future. With the progress they're making, I am confident they will find a cure for this disease. Never give up, always think positive no matter what, and enjoy your life day by day.

"Life is not measured by the breaths we take but by the moments that take our breath away."

Blue Skies, Sunny Days, Healthy Tomorrows

Jan Tarantino

Here is my story. I had a hysterectomy in August, 1996 and learned that I had stage IV ovarian cancer with a large tumor on the liver as well. When the doctor told my husband and me I might only have a couple of years left, I fell apart. The doctor said even with chemo that might be all the time I would have.

I began chemo shortly after surgery and I decided I would be as strong as I could possibly be. I cried a lot and was very depressed at first, but something made me get tough with it all and it worked. My doctor says it's that getting tough that helped me. I believe he's right. I told myself I would beat my ovarian cancer (ovac) and if God would help me and give me the strength I would find a way to help others have faith and be strong. I do a lot of that on the Johns Hopkins Ovac Support Board. It is the best. We share and care so much. This quote is just one among many that we share on our support board: "Friends are like angels who lift us to our feet when our wings have trouble remembering to fly."

I know how true that is from my own experiences with cancer. I chose to be around people who were just there for me and did not ask a lot of questions. One dear friend always gave me hope and was there to listen when I needed someone. She came to see me a week after my hysterectomy. She brought enough food for days for hubby and me and made me eat. Bless her. I will never forget her kindnesses. As for hubby, he was always there for me and took over the housekeeping and all. He learned to do laundry pretty quickly; he sat with me through chemo treatments.

As for my post cancer, I of course keep up with my follow-up care; do the best I can to help others that might be in need of support; and always keep humor in my life because laughter IS really the best medicine.

Blue skies, sunny days and healthy tomorrows! Keeping the faith, I am very thankful. Be well and take care of you.

"I've had cancer 6 times. Don't stereotype me!"

Genetic Predisposition

Rick Ecalono

Cancer runs in our family, clear and simple. At 28, I was the first in my family to be diagnosed—bladder cancer, an old man's disease. In 1982 my father, brother Buddy and I all came down with cancer. For my dad and brother it was colon cancer. Buddy, told that he would live to be an old man, died less then 2 years later in 1984 at the age of 37. My father, who was given 6 months to live, died in 2000—a true cancer survivor. In 1999 my younger brother John came down with colon cancer and I came down with my third cancer—ureter.

By the time I was 40, I had not only buried my brother, but also beat back three bladder cancers and found myself facing colon cancer. It started to seem like a lot more than coincidence when I was diagnosed. I had to ask myself: "Could it be part of our genetic makeup like blue eyes?" "Are my remaining three sisters and one brother, my kids and theirs on a collision course with cancer?" And boy was I the unlikely messenger of a "wake up and fly right" strategy for our family.

I was no angel. In fact, in the 1980s with my money-as-God invincible attitude, many in the family saw me as an inconsiderate, self-absorbed and detached egotist. The early cancers didn't change that. They just made me work harder, earn more, and leave the rearing of our children to my wife. I was impatient, hard and judgmental. My wife pointed out that my illnesses should have brought us closer together; not driven us further apart. It's no wonder our marriage ended in divorce in 1991.

Things changed dramatically though with my colon cancer. Money and business took a back seat to my need to know if a bad gene was the cause of my cancer and my brother's death and if it meant cancer was lurking and waiting to attack the rest of my family. I became the driving force in convincing my siblings to participate in an NIH study on colon cancer in families. On a warm day in April of 1997, we showed up at NIH bringing with us an old family remedy for dealing with sorrow and nervousness: laughter. The joking and the kidding, interspersed with some betting on who was going to have the problem gene, filled the time between each of our private consultations.

I also made sure the next generation—my kids and my nieces and nephews—understood the consequences of having the gene. If they tested positive they had an 85% chance of getting colon cancer. But with early and aggressive treatment, they were likely to enjoy long and productive lives. I urged—even begged—all in my family to be tested.

Most of the younger generation chose not to be tested, but fortunately, my pestering made a difference. The possibility of inheriting the trait made my kids and my nieces and nephews more aware of the environmental factors that contribute to cancer—attitude, eating habits and stress. Many now reach for a second stalk of broccoli rather than a chocolate bar. Others have joined religious groups that don't permit drinking or smoking.

For myself, I decided cancer wasn't going to stop me. I was

going to stay on top of it and beat it. My motto: "I've had cancer six times. Don't stereotype me." I have shared my story with lawmakers on Capitol Hill, urging that the right to privacy be ensured for those who receive genetic testing. I've also spoken around the country about what it feels like to live with a faulty gene. My hope is that my story will help an ever growing number of people as more and more diseases become linked to human genes. I know for sure it's what I'm supposed to do and that I'll be doing it for a long time to come.

*"Let the skies flood you with liquid sunshine...
Nourishing you with the knowledge of truth."*

Colors of Life

Jeanne Bonine

In many ways my career as a successful print artist, sprung out of necessity in 1990. I chose to walk away with nothing from my second marriage as college tuitions for my two teenage boys loomed heavy. The art world was abuzz with the success of limited edition prints and I believed I could be a part of that success. I marched into a printer's office and said: "You don't know me or my work from beans. I have no money, but I'd like to print this piece. Give me 60 days and I'll pay you back." And I did. It was no coincidence that the painting I chose to have made into a print was called "Once Upon A Dream;" and during the next four years my dream to be an accepted print artist did indeed come true.

In the midst of this wonderful career, I was diagnosed with cancer in 1994. I had just purchased a home in Cave Creek, Arizona when I was hit with the news. In this beautiful Sonoran desert location, my work began to take on the qualities of both my inner journey and the Arizona landscape. I also began to write a philosophical message to accompany each image.

I never for a moment forgot that I was in a battle for my life and that loving energy, not fear, was the only weapon that would subdue this enemy. I did beautiful things for myself like taking nice baths. On the way to radiation treatments I would breathe in the beauty of nature and feel its healing graces. All of these things, plus wonderful medical care worked.

After more than ten years, I'm still here. Today, life is sweet and successful at every level. I continue to get emotionally lost in flowers. They are a place for my mind to go. My paintings of flowers were soft and light until after my challenge with cancer. Now the colors are strong because I am stronger myself.

My wonderful home, my flower gardens, the company of family and friends make me happy and bring me peace. My boys whom I worried about so much during my divorce and my illness are my pride and joy. My four grandkids are just where I want them, close to my heart.

For all going through the cancer journey, I'd like to share a portion of a poem I wrote called "Garden of Life:"

Let the earth cradle you in the soil of wisdom,
Rocking you to sleep through its selfless rhythm.
Let the skies flood you with liquid sunshine…
Nourishing you with the knowledge of truth.
Lie there in the bed of cosmic sweetness,
Until your heart has learned to sing and the sound has
Awakened you to life.

I Am A Survivor

I am a survivor. Cancer is my foe.
Although it waits most patiently. I'm not ready to go.

Many are the sunsets my eyes have yet to see.
A lovely rose, a blissful bird whose song enraptures me.

I am a survivor. There's still so much to do!
To taste, to feel, to see, to hear, time to spend with you.

I wear no badge of courage. My scars I would not bare.
But locked deep down inside, a memory lingers there.

For I am a survivor, I bless each precious day.
And capture every fleeting moment that life has sent my way.

Tranquility surrounds me when gentle breezes blow.
Quite like the touch of kindness from whom I love so.

I am a survivor. There's so much need of me.
And what I have to offer, I'll do graciously.

My door will always open, if I can lend an ear.
To soothe a hurt, to ease a pain, to calm a deepest fear.

I am a survivor. Death has no claim on me.
I know someday it will come my time and I'll go gallantly.

But 'til then, I am a survivor, there's too much life to live,
Time for caring, time for sharing; all that love to give!

Yes, I am a survivor. You'll recognize my smile.
You see, I am free just to be me, knowing all the while.

I am a survivor

RESEARCH AND RESOURCE SECTION

Websites from authors of the stories:

www.at-face-value.com - Terry Healey.
www.angelfire.com/ct3/survivorofcancer - Vincent Sussman
http://www.senseofsecurity.org - Vickie Tosher
www.inspirezone.org - Tony Presley
www.globalwalk.org - Debi Linker
www.celebrateloveandlife.com - Sam Golden
www.cybermage.netgate.net - Mike Lachtanski
www.cllf.org - Cammy Lee Leukemia Foundation
www.cancerguide.org - Steve Dunn
www.healthyspirits.com - Linda Kedy
www.cancermed.com - Paul Leverett
www.stepsforliving.org - Matthew Zachary
www.onelifeusa.com - Jana Brabec
www.jeannebonine.com - Jeanne Bonine

Cancer Organizations/Websites:

Alliance for Lung Cancer
P.O. Box 849
Vancouver, WA 98666
800-298-2436
info@alcase.org
http://www.alcase.org

The Alliance for Lung Cancer Advocacy, Support, and Education (ALCASE) is the only not-for-profit organization dedicated solely to helping those living with lung cancer improve the quality of their lives through advocacy, support, and education.

American Brain Tumor Association
2720 River Road, Suite 146
Des Plains, IL 60018-4110
800-886-2282
info@abta.org
http://www.abta.org

The American Brain Tumor Association exists to eliminate brain tumors through research and to meet the needs of brain tumor patients and their families. The website contains written information about specific brain tumors, treatments and clinical trials; patient conferences, phone line, newsletter, **The Message Line;** funds research.

American Cancer Society
1599 Clifton Road, NE
Atlanta, GA 30329
1-800-ACS-2345 - Cancer Information Specialists are available 24 hours a day to answer your questions.
www.cancer.org

Medical information, treatment decision tools, news updates, and support resources. You can also read about survivors' experiences, find hope, and inspire others.

American Cancer Society is the nationwide community-based voluntary health organization dedicated to eliminating cancer as a major health problem by preventing cancer, saving lives, and diminishing suffering from cancer, through research, education, advocacy, and service.

American Institute for Cancer Research
1759 R Street NW
Washington, DC 20069
202-328-7744
www.aicr.org

AICR is the cancer charity that fosters research on diet and cancer prevention and educates the public about the results.

American Lung Association
61 Broadway, 6th Floor
NY, NY 10006
212-315-8700
www.lungusa.org

The American Lung Association today fights lung disease in all its forms, with special emphasis on asthma, tobacco control and environmental health. The American Lung Association has many programs and strategies for fighting lung disease.

Breast Cancer Survivor Foundation
333 S. State Street
Suite V #314
Lake Oswego, OR 97034
503-502-6776
info@breastcancersurvivors.org
www.breastcancersurvivors.org

The Breast Cancer Survivors Foundation (an Oregon-based nonprofit corporation), was established in 2000 by Andrea Leonard-Bruno to help the millions of survivors who, like her mother, are trying to regain control of their lives and bodies. The mission of the foundation is to focus on the survivors' needs and not just the disease. Dedicated to improving the quality of life of breast cancer survivors and their families through education, postoperative exercise programs, research grants, fund-raising, discussion forums and outreach programs.

The Brain Tumor Society
124 Watertown Street, Suite 3-H
Watertown, MA 02472
1-800-770-TBTS (8287)
617-924-9997
info@tbts.org
www.tbts.org

The Brain Tumor Society exists to find a cure for brain tumors. It strives to improve the quality of life of brain tumor patients and their families. It disseminates educational information and provides access to psycho-social support. It raises funds to advance carefully selected scientific research projects, improve clinical care and find a cure.

Cancer Care, Inc.
275 Seventh Avenue
New York, NY 10001
800-813-HOPE or 212-712-8080
info@cancercare.org
www.cancercare.org

Cancer Care is a national non-profit organization whose mission is to provide free professional help to people with all cancers through counseling, education, information and referral and direct financial assistance.

Cancer Hope Network
Two North Road
Chester, NJ 07930
877-467-3638 (1-877-HOPENET)
info@cancerhopenetwork.org
www.cancerhopenetwork.org

The Cancer Hope Network provides individual support to cancer patients and their families by matching them with trained volunteers who have undergone and recovered from a similar cancer experience. Such matches are based on the type and stage of cancer, treatments used, side effects experienced, and other factors.

Cancer Information and Counseling Line (CICL)
(a service of the AMC Cancer Research Center)
1600 Pierce Street
Denver, CO 80214
1-800-525-3777
cicl@amc.org
www.amc.org

The CICL, part of the Psychosocial Program of the AMC Cancer Research Center, is a toll-free telephone service for patients, their family members and friends, cancer survivors, and the general public. Professional counselors provide up-to-date medical information, emotional support through short-term counseling, and resource referrals to callers nationwide between the hours of 9:00 a.m. and 5:00 p.m. MT. Individuals may also submit questions about cancer and request resources via e-mail.

Cancer Research and Prevention Foundation
Suite 500
1600 Duke Street
Alexandria, VA 22314
703-836-4412
1-800-227-2732 (1-800-227-CRFA)
info@preventcancer.org
www.preventcancer.org

The Cancer Research Foundation of America seeks to prevent cancer by funding research and providing educational materials on early detection and nutrition.

Clinical Trials and Noteworthy Treatments for Brain Tumors
Musella Foundation For Brain Tumor
Research & Information
1100 Peninsula Blvd.
Hewlett, NY 11557
musella@virtualtrials.com
www.virtualtrials.com

A web site which supplies information on the treatments available for brain tumors, with a focus on new and/or experimental treatments.

Colon Cancer Alliance (CCA)
175 Ninth Avenue
New York, NY 10011
1-877-422-2030
info@ccalliance.org
www.ccalliance.org

The Colon Cancer Alliance brings the voice of survivors to battle colorectal cancer through patient support, education, research and advocacy.

Colorectal Cancer Network
P.O. Box 182
Kensington, MD 20895-0182
301-879-1500
ccnetwork@colorectal-cancer.net
www.colorectal-cancer.net

The Colorectal Cancer Network is a national advocacy group that raises public awareness about colorectal cancer and provides support services to colorectal cancer patients and their families, friends and caregivers. Services include support groups; an Internet chat room; e-mail listservs for survivors, caregivers and advocates; hospital visitation programs; and a "One on One" service that connects newly diagnosed individuals with long-term survivors. The Network also provides literature on screening, diagnosis, treatment and supportive care for colorectal cancer.

Gilda's Club® Worldwide
Suite 1402
322 Eighth Avenue
New York, NY 10001
1-888-445-3248 (1-888-GILDA-4-U)
info@gildasclub.org
www.gildasclub.org

The mission of Gilda's Club is to provide places where men, women and children with cancer and their families and friends join with others to build social and emotional support as a supplement to medical care. Free of charge and non-profit, Gilda's Clubs offer support and networking groups, lectures, workshops and social events in a nonresidential, home-like setting.

Lance Armstrong Foundation (LAF)
Post Office Box 161150
Austin, TX 78716-1150
512-236-8820
www.laf.org

The Lance Armstrong Foundation (LAF) exists to enhance the quality of life for those living with, through and beyond cancer. Founded in 1997 by cancer survivor and champion cyclist Lance Armstrong, the LAF seeks to promote the optimal physical, psychological, social recovery and care of cancer survivors and their loved ones. The LAF works to define, refine and improve services for cancer survivors and to facilitate the delivery of those services—with a large dose of hope—to patients, their families and other loved ones touched by the disease.

Leukemia and Lymphoma Society
1311 Mamaroneck Ave.
White Plains, NY 10605
914-949-5213
e-mail: infocenter@leukemia.org
www.leukemia-lymphoma.org

The Leukemia and Lymphoma Society's mission is to cure leukemia, lymphoma, Hodgkin's disease and myeloma, and to improve the quality of life of patients and their families. The Society has dedicated itself to being one of the top-rated voluntary health agencies in terms of dollars that directly fund our mission.

Lymphoma Research Foundation
8800 Venice Blvd. Suite 207
Los Angeles, CA 90034
310-204-7040
e-mail: lrfa@aol.com
www.lymphoma.org

The Lymphoma Research Foundation (LRF) is the nation's largest lymphoma-focused voluntary health organization devoted exclusively to funding lymphoma research and providing patients and healthcare professionals with critical information on the disease. LRF's mission is to eradicate lymphoma and serve those touched by the disease.

National Brain Tumor Foundation
414 Thirteenth Street, Suite 700
Oakland, CA 94612-2603
Brain Tumor Information Line: 800-934-CURE (2873)
www.braintumor.org

NBTF is a national non-profit health organization dedicated to providing information and support for brain tumor patients, family members and healthcare professionals, while supporting innovative research into better treatment options and a cure for brain tumors.

National Cancer Institute
Building 31, Room 10A24
Bethesda, MD 20892
Cancer Information Service and Physician Data Query
1-800-4CANCER
http://cis.nci.nih.gov

The National Cancer Institute's Cancer Information Service, provides the latest and most accurate cancer information to patients, their families, the public and health professionals. Through its network of regional offices, the CIS serves the United States, Puerto Rico, the U.S. Virgin Islands, and the Pacific Islands.

The National Cancer Institute (NCI) is a component of the National Institutes of Health (NIH), one of eight agencies that compose the Public Health Service (PHS) in the Department of Health and Human Services (DHHS). The NCI, established under the National Cancer Act of 1937, is the Federal Government's principal agency for cancer research and training. The National Cancer Act of 1971 broadened the scope and responsibilities of the NCI and created the National Cancer Program. Over the years, legislative amendments have maintained the NCI authorities and responsibilities and added new information dissemination mandates as well as a requirement to assess the incorporation of state-of-the-art cancer treatments into clinical practice. The National Cancer Institute coordinates the National Cancer Program, which conducts and supports research, training, health information dissemination, and other programs with respect to the cause, diagnosis, prevention, and treatment of cancer, rehabilitation from cancer, and the continuing care of cancer patients and the families of cancer patients.

National Coalition for Cancer Survivorship
Suite 770
1010 Wayne Avenue
Silver Springs, MD 20910-5600
1-877-622-7937 (1-877-NCCS-YES)
info@canceradvocacy.org
www.canceradvocacy.org

The National Coalition for Cancer Survivorship (NCCS) is the only survivor-led advocacy organization working exclusively on behalf of this country's more than 9 million cancer survivors and the millions more touched by this disease. Founded in 1986, NCCS continues to lead the cancer survivorship movement. By educating all those affected by cancer and speaking out on issues related to quality cancer care, NCCS is empowering every survivor.

National Marrow Donor Program (NMDP)
Suite 500
3001 Broadway Street, NE.
Minneapolis, MN 55413-1753
800-627-7692 (800-MARROW-2)
888-999-6743 (Office of Patient Advocacy)
www.marrow.org

The National Marrow Donor Program (NMDP), which is funded by the Federal Government, was created to improve the effectiveness of the search for bone marrow donors. It keeps a registry of potential bone marrow donors and provides free information on bone marrow transplantation, peripheral blood stem cell transplant, and unrelated donor stem cell transplant, including the use of umbilical cord blood. The NMDP's Office of Patient Advocacy assists transplant patients and their physicians through the donor search and transplant process by providing information, referrals, support, and advocacy.

National Ovarian Cancer Coalition, Inc.
500 NE Spanish River Boulevard, Suite 8
Boca Raton, FL 33431
1-888-OVARIAN
NOCC@ovarian.org
www.ovarian.org

The mission is to raise awareness about ovarian cancer and to promote education about this disease. By dispelling myths and misunderstandings, the coalition is committed to improve the overall survival rate and quality of life for women with ovarian cancer.

OncoLink
Abramson Cancer Center of the University of Pennsylvania
3400 Spruce Street - 2 Donner
Philadelphia, PA 19104-4283
contact@oncolink.com
www.oncolink.org

OncoLink was founded in 1994 by Penn cancer specialists with a mission to help cancer patients, families, health care professionals and the general public get accurate cancer-related information at no charge. Through OncoLink you can get comprehensive information about specific types of cancer, updates on cancer treatments and news about research advances. Information is updated everyday and provides information at various levels, from introductory to in-depth.

Patient Advocate Foundation (PAF)
Suite B
753 Thimble Shoals Boulevard
Newport News, VA 23606
800-532-5274
help@patientadvocate.org
www.patientadvocate.org

Patient Advocate Foundation is a national non-profit organization that serves as an active liaison between the patient and their insurer, employer and/or creditors to resolve insurance, job retention and/or debt crisis matters relative to their diagnosis through case managers, doctors and attorneys. Patient Advocate Foundation seeks to safeguard patients through effective mediation assuring access to care, maintenance of employment and preservation of their financial stability.

Prostate Cancer Foundation
1250 Fourth Street
Santa Monica, CA 90401
800-757-2873 (800-757-CURE)
info@prostatecancerfoundation.org
www.prostatecancerfoundation.org/

The Prostate Cancer Foundation (PCF) is the world's largest philanthropy supporting prostate cancer research. PCF was founded in 1993 with an urgent mission: to find better treatments and a cure for advanced prostate cancer. PCF reaches out to private industry, the patient advocacy community and government research institutions and has established a system that encourages collaboration, reduces bureaucracy and speeds the process of discovery. These partnerships provide a model to speed the cure for prostate cancer - and all cancers.

R. A. Bloch Cancer Foundation, Inc.
4400 Main Street
Kansas City, MO 64111
816-932-8453 (816-WE-BUILD)
800-433-0464
hotline@hrblock.com
www.blochcancer.org

The R. A. Bloch Cancer Foundation matches newly diagnosed cancer patients with trained, home-based volunteers who have been treated for the same type of cancer. They also distribute informational materials, including a multidisciplinary list of institutions that offer second opinions. Information is available in Spanish.

Sisters Network Inc.
National Headquarters
8787 Woodway Drive - Suite 4206
Houston, TX 77063
713-781-0255
sisnet4@aol.com

Sisters Network is committed to increasing local and national attention to the devastating impact that breast cancer has in the African American Community.

Support for People with Oral and Head and Neck Cancer (SPOHNC)
Post Office Box 53
Locust Valley, NY 11560-0053
1-800-377-0928
info@spohnc.org
www.spohnc.org

The SPOHNC is a self-help organization that serves oral and head and neck cancer patients, survivors, and their families. The organization offers support group meetings, information, newsletters, and teleconferences. The SPOHNC also offers a "Survivor to Survivor" network which pairs survivors or their family members with volunteers who have had a similar diagnosis and treatment program. Volunteers offer survivors information, support, hope and encouragement.

Susan G. Komen Foundation
Headquarters
5005 LBJ Freeway, Suite 250
Dallas, TX 75244
972-855-1600
HelpLine: 800 I'M AWARE

For more than 20 years, the Susan G. Komen Breast Cancer Foundation has been a global leader in the fight against breast cancer through its support of innovative research and community-based outreach programs. Working through a network of U.S. and international affiliates and events like the Komen Race for the Cure®, the Komen Foundation is fighting to eradicate breast cancer as a life-threatening disease by funding research grants and supporting education, screening and treatment projects in communities around the world.

Testicular Cancer Resource Center
The Testicular Cancer Resource Center is a charitable organization devoted to helping people understand testicular and extragonadal germ cell tumors. Specifically, we provide accurate and timely information about these tumors and their treatment to anyone and everyone interested. We have information for patients, caregivers, family, friends, and physicians. www.tcrc.acor.org

Thyroid Cancer Survivors' Association, Inc.
PO Box 1545
New York, NY 10159-1545
1-877-588-7904
www.thyca@thyca.org

Thyroid Cancer Survivors' Association, Inc. is an all-volunteer, non-profit organization of thyroid cancer survivors, family members and health care professionals. We are dedicated to support, education, and communication for thyroid cancer survivors, their families and friends.

Us TOO International, Inc.
Prostate Cancer Support Groups
5003 Fairview Avenue
Downers Grove, IL 60515
630-795-1002
PCa Support Hotline: 800-80-Us TOO (800-808-7866)
ustoo@ustoo.org

Us TOO is a 501(c)(3) charitable/not-for-profit organization representing the needs of prostate cancer survivors, their families, men at risk, and health care providers, serving our chapters and their members, our supporters, constituencies, patient communities and the health care/research communities. Us TOO accomplishes this by providing leadership through proactive education and publications, public awareness/outreach, and patient/family support networking programs as well as by taking proactive positions supporting more effective screening, enhanced treatment options and increased funding for prostate cancer research.

Vital Options International, Inc.
15821 Ventura Blvd., Suite 645
Encino, CA 91436-2946
1-818-788-5225
info@vitaloptions.org

Vital Options® International TeleSupport® Cancer Network is a not-for-profit cancer communications, support and advocacy organization whose mission is to facilitate a global cancer dialogue by using communications technology to reach every person touched by cancer.

WINGS
Texas Wings
4438 Centerview Dr.
Suite 109
San Antonio, TX 78228
210-9469464
tjones@texaswings.org

Texas Wings (Women Involved in Nurturing, Giving, Sharing) is a non-profit Texas Corporation whose mission is to bring top quality breast care.

Y-ME National Breast Cancer Organization
212 W. Van Buren, Suite 1000
Chicago, IL 60607-3908
1-800-221-2141 (English)*
1-800-986-9505 (Español)

The mission of Y-ME National Breast Cancer Organization is to ensure, through information, empowerment and peer support, that no one faces breast cancer alone.

Callers can be matched with a survivor, patient and/or supporter who have had a similar experience with breast cancer.
*Interpreters available in 150 languages

Young Survival Coalition
155 6th Avenue, 10th Floor
New York, NY 10013
212-206-6610
info@youngsurvival.org
www.youngsurvival.org

The Young Survival Coalition (YSC) is the only international, non-profit network of breast cancer survivors and supporters dedicated to the concerns and issues that are unique to young women and breast cancer. Through action, advocacy and awareness, the YSC seeks to educate the medical, research, breast cancer and legislative communities and to persuade them to address breast cancer in women 40 and under. The YSC also serves as a point of contact for young women living with breast cancer.

Special Programs for Cancer Patients

American Cancer Society – Reach to Recovery

The American Cancer Society's Reach to Recovery program has been helping breast cancer patients (female and male) cope with their breast cancer experience for more than 30 years. This experience begins at the moment someone is faced with the possibility of a breast cancer diagnosis and continues throughout the entire period that breast cancer remains a personal concern.

Talking with a specially trained Reach to Recovery volunteer at this time can provide a measure of comfort and an opportunity for emotional grounding and informed decision-making. Volunteers are breast cancer survivors who give patients and family members an opportunity to express feelings, verbalize fears and concerns, and ask questions of someone who is knowledgeable and level-headed. Most importantly, Reach to Recovery volunteers offer understanding, support, and hope because they themselves have survived breast cancer and gone on to live normal, productive lives.

American Cancer Society – Cancer Survivor Network

Free support network, created by and for cancer survivors and loved ones, on the web or phone, 24 hours a day. On the web, get support from others like you via personal homepages, discussions, chats, personal stories, talk shows, and more. Stories and shows are also available free at 1-877-333-HOPE.

Cancer Survivors Network (www.acscsn.org)

This is both a telephone and Web-based service for cancer survivors, their families, caregivers, and friends. The telephone component (1-877-333-HOPE) provides survivors and families access to pre-recorded discussions. The Web-based component offers live online chat sessions, virtual support groups, pre-recorded talk shows, and personal stories.

American Cancer Society – Look Good... Feel Better

The Look Good...Feel Better program is a community-based, free, national service that teaches female cancer patients beauty techniques to help restore their appearance and self-image during chemotherapy and radiation treatments.

American Cancer Society – I Can Cope

I Can Cope is an educational program provided in a supportive environment for adults with cancer and their loved ones. The program offers several courses that are designed to help participants cope with their cancer experience by increasing their knowledge, positive attitude, and skills.

Individuals who know more about their disease can make informed decisions with their doctors, becoming partners on their treatment teams. I Can Cope can help you and your family work through the feelings of fear and frustration that so often come with a cancer diagnosis. The program is conducted by trained healthcare professionals, often with hospital co-sponsorship.

The program offers straightforward cancer information and answers to questions about human anatomy, cancer development, diagnosis, treatment, side effects, new research, communication, emotions, sexuality, self-esteem, and community resources. The program also provides information, encouragement, and practical hints through presentations and class discussions. All courses are free.

American Cancer Society – Man to Man

The Man to Man program helps men cope with prostate cancer by providing community-based education and support to patients and their family members. In addition, Man to Man plays an important role in community education about prostate cancer; it encourages men and health care professionals to actively consider screening for prostate cancer appropriate to each man's age and risk for the disease.

A major part of the program is the self-help and/or support group. Volunteers organize free monthly meetings where speakers and participants learn about and discuss information about prostate cancer, treatment, side effects and how to cope with the disease and its treatment.

Recommended Books, Magazines and Audio Tapes:

American Cancer Society Consumer Guide to Cancer Drugs, Second Edition
Published by the American Cancer Society and Jones and Bartlett Publishers

At Face Value by Terry Healey
A successful marketing consultant and cancer survivor shares his story and provides a source of strength and hope for life's challenges and adversities.

Awaken the Healer Within (Prime Books Anthologies)
Author(s): Billauer, Dr. Michael; Billauer, Madonna; Nani, Tomas; Lamarche, Dr. Gilles A.; Raymer, Ann; Clapp W. Lawrence; Cover/ACP DESIGNS, Mark Victor Hansen

Focuses on the emotional aspects of healing, and he coaches men suffering from prostate problems, including cancer.

Breast Cancer Prevention Diet: The Powerful Foods, Supplements, and Drugs That Can Change Your Life
by Dr. Bob Arnot

Cancer as a Turning Point by Laurence LeShan
Handbook for people with cancer, their families and health professionals.

Cancer Clinical Trials by Robert Finn
He tells you everything you need to know about finding and evaluating experimental cancer treatments. While he does not recommend any specific treatments, he believes that everyone with a diagnosis of cancer owes it to themselves to evaluate available clinical trials along with other treatment options.

Cancer in the Family
Helping Children Cope with a Parent's Illness
Published by the American Cancer Society

Coping With Cancer is America's consumer magazine for people whose lives have been touched by cancer™. Now in its 18th year of providing knowledge, hope and inspiration, its readers include cancer patients (survivors) and their families, caregivers, healthcare teams and support group leaders. www.copingmag.com

Dancing With the Diagnosis: Steps for Taking the Lead When Facing Cancer by Michelle Waters
A guide for gaining control, creating clear communication, and making sense of life after you or someone you love is diagnosed with cancer.

***Dr. Susan Love's Breast Book* (A Merloyd Lawrence Book)**
by Susan M. Love

Dreamwalk, A Survivor's Journey Through Breast Cancer
by Rachael Clearwater
A short, easily readable account of one woman's breast cancer ordeal from diagnosis, through treatment and into the awareness of the present moment. The pages are filled with encouragement and the sense of a positive outcome.

Getting Well Again by O. Carl Simonton, M.D.
The bestselling classic about the Simontons' revolutionary life-saving self-awareness techniques. Released: 01 April, 1992.

Head First: The Biology of Hope and the Healing Power of the Human Spirit by Norman Cousins
Cousins connects personal experience with scientific research to make a compelling case for the healing power of positive emotions.

It's Not About the Bike: My Journey Back to Life by Lance Armstrong, Sally Jenkins (Contributor)

The Journey Through Cancer: An Oncologist's Seven-Level Program for Healing and Transforming the Whole Person by Jeremy R. Geffen

Love, Medicine and Miracles: Lessons Learned about Self-Healing from a Surgeon's Experience with Exceptional Patients by Bernie S. Siegel

Prostate Health in 90 Days...Without Drugs or Surgery by Dr. Larry Clapp
Offers men new options for the prevention and treatment of prostate problems.

Self-Esteem Affirmations: Motivational Affirmations for Building Confidence and Recognizing Self-Worth Self-Esteem Affirmations by Louise Hay

PAUL E. HUFF

Paul is President of Paul Huff International, a speaking and training company dedicated to creating and delivering dynamic information, powerful programs and practical tools of the highest quality that consistently transform the beliefs, behaviors and results people and organizations need to create success that lasts a lifetime.

Paul works with many of America's Fortune 1000 companies involved in virtually every industry. Tens of thousands of people in more than 13 nations have benefited from the humor, energy, and passion of Paul Huff's insightful writings, seminars, keynotes and audio recordings. Organizations and associations want Paul on their team because he facilitates bottom-line results time and time again.

Before launching his own business as a sought-after speaker, seminar leader and executive coach, Paul spent 27 successful years as a leader in the financial services industry. In the financial world, Paul served as a senior vice president of First Union Home Equity Corporation, where he was the first recipient of the coveted President's Award for Excellence. He consistently broke sales, productivity and operational records, and was a key leader in many award-winning quality initiatives.

Paul realized through speaking to large groups that he was able to touch even more lives with his message, and take his passion for helping people to a new level. Today, Paul combines his solid business background with passion-fired skills in teaching both individuals and organizations to achieve unprecedented performance with ease and joy. He specializes in the area of personal and professional development, sales, teambuilding, leadership and customer service.

Paul is also the author of the book *Imagination Always Wins!*

Paul is a big man, with a big heart, a big spirit and a big message. He is an inspiration to all who seek to live happier, more productive and more meaningful lives. Paul's loss of his first wife to cancer has made him relentlessly passionate about bringing to fruition this much needed book for those with cancer and those who care about them.

For more details on Paul and the inspiring work he does for the business community visit www.paulhuff.com.